EVERYDAY
ITALIAN
COOKBOOK

WILLIAMS
SONOMA
CALIFORNIA

WILLIAMS
SONOMA
CALIFORNIA

EVERYDAY
ITALIAN
COOKBOOK

90+ FAVORITE RECIPES FOR LA CUCINA ITALIANA

DOMENICA MARCHETTI

weldon**owen**

CONTENTS

PIZZA | FOCACCIA

MEAT | FISH

VEGETABLES | EGGS

DOLCI | SWEETS

INTRODUCTION

In 2021, my husband and I bought a small house at the top of a medieval town in Abruzzo, Italy. We were swayed by the thick wood beams of the living room ceiling and by the view from the postage-stamp terrace over crooked terra-cotta-tiled rooftops and soft rolling hills out to the Adriatic Sea.

My mom was born and raised in Abruzzo, a region blessed with both mountains and coastline, and as a girl I spent many summers sunbathing on the beach and exploring the curvy mountain roads with my family and friends. I was thrilled to once again have a place here to call home.

In reality, the house needs work: furniture, new bathrooms, a fresh coat of paint. But the kitchen is small and functional, and it suits me fine. More and more, I find myself gravitating toward everyday Italian cooking, and for that you don't need a fancy kitchen. Instead, I rely on a few good pots and pans and on recipes that I know will work time after time. I love making dishes that get their "wow" factor from fresh seasonal ingredients and good pantry staples, rather than from overwrought sauces or complicated techniques.

This book reflects my philosophy that simple everyday food is the best food, a joy to make and to eat. Among the recipes are Bucatini Cacio e Pepe, fat noodles tossed in a creamy sauce of sheep's milk cheese and copious amounts of freshly ground pepper; savory, tender Chicken Ricotta Meatballs in Tomato Sauce; Aeolian Bread Salad enriched with tuna, potatoes, and olives; and Dark Chocolate Panna Cotta with Amarena Cherries, as dreamy as it sounds.

There are plenty more recipes for you to explore. These are dishes I'm proud to set out for family and friends to enjoy. It's my hope that you'll enjoy them as much as we do.

A Trio of Amaretti, page 152

Chocolate Almond Torte, page 166

SPUNTINI

APERITIVI

Bread with Olive Oil and Tomatoes

Pane, olio e pomodoro was my favorite summer snack growing up, and it remains so today. *The one thing to remember is that the quality of ingredients is everything: country bread with a sturdy crust and a big, open crumb; new-harvest olive oil, one that conjures artichokes and bites the back of your throat; and ripe red tomatoes with plenty of savory juices.*

8 slices coarse country bread

2 small cloves garlic, lightly crushed

2–3 tomatoes, halved

Extra-virgin olive oil, for drizzling (see Cook's Note)

Flaky sea salt

Leaves from 1 fresh basil sprig for garnish

MAKES 4 SERVINGS

Arrange the bread slices in a single layer on a large platter and rub the top surfaces with the garlic. Rub the tomato halves, cut side down, on each slice, squeezing some of the flesh out of the tomato and onto the bread. Be as messy as you like. Drizzle the oil on top, a little or a lot, and sprinkle with salt. Garnish with the basil and serve.

COOK'S NOTE

I keep a selection of olive oils, mostly from small producers, in my pantry. I use more mild-flavored oil, or oil from the previous year's harvest, for cooking, and more assertive, grassy oil , or *olio nuovo*, for drizzling on soups and dressing salads. Freshly pressed oil is a luxury worth splurging on once a year for its "green" tomato flavor and peppery bite.

Fresh Fig "Flowers" with Gorgonzola, Thyme, and Honey

I have a small but prolific Brown Turkey fig tree in my backyard that produces a generous crop of reddish-purple fruits in late summer. The figs are small and rather plain, and I use most of them to make jam. But when I find good, large plump ones, I make this easy, elegant antipasto. Use any good fresh fig, whether green or purple.

12 large, ripe fresh figs

Several fresh unblemished fig leaves, for lining the platter (optional)

¼ lb (115 g) salty cheese, such as Gorgonzola, Stilton, semisoft pecorino, or feta, crumbled or cut into smallish cubes

Leaves from a few fresh thyme sprigs, for garnish

2–3 tablespoons runny honey

MAKES 6 SERVINGS

Remove the stem from each fig. Using a sharp knife, and starting at the stem end, cut each fig lengthwise into quarters, taking care not to cut all the way to the bottom. (This will allow each fig to open like a flower while remaining intact.) If using the fig leaves, line a platter with them. Arrange the figs on the platter.

Place an equal amount of the cheese in the center of each fig. Garnish each fig with a pinch of thyme leaves. Drizzle the honey evenly over the figs and serve.

Fried Sage Leaves and Flowers

Battered and fried sage leaves look lacy and delicate, but they are actually quite rich, so only three or four per person are needed. If you happen to grow sage in your garden, you can also fry the purple flower heads, which have a lovely, subtle flavor and look pretty on the plate. You'll have leftover batter, as only a small amount is needed to coat the leaves. Refrigerate the remainder in an airtight container for up to two days and use it to fry zucchini slices and zucchini blossoms, broccoli or cauliflower florets, or anything that strikes your fancy. Fried sage leaves are best served hot, so pass them around as soon as all of them are out of the oil.

1 cup (125 g) unbleached all-purpose flour

Fine sea salt

1 cup (240 ml) sparkling water

1 large egg, lightly beaten

Sunflower or other neutral oil, for frying

24 large, unblemished fresh sage leaves with stem attached

Sage flowers with stem attached (optional)

MAKES 6–8 SERVINGS

In a bowl, combine the flour and ½ teaspoon salt. Whisk in the water, mixing well to avoid lumps. Add the egg and whisk until incorporated. Set aside.

Line a plate with paper towels and set it near the stove. Pour the oil to a depth of ½ inch (12 mm) into a frying pan and heat over medium-high heat until the oil shimmers. It is ready when a small bead of batter dropped into it sizzles and immediately floats to the surface. Fry the sage leaves in batches: Hold a leaf by its stem and dip it into the batter, letting the excess drip off, then gently drop the leaf into the oil. Add as many dipped leaves as will fit comfortably in the pan without crowding. Fry until light golden on the underside, 1–2 minutes. Using a fork or tongs, gently turn the leaves and fry on the other side for 1–2 minutes longer. Use a skimmer or slotted spoon to transfer the fried leaves to the towel-lined plate. Continue to batter and fry the sage leaves until all the leaves are fried. If using sage flowers, dip and fry them the same way.

Lightly season the leaves and flowers (if using) with salt and serve.

Fried Eggplant "Sandwiches" with Prosciutto Cotto, Mozzarella, and Rosemary

My friend Tina Prestia is an expat living in Italy. When I went to visit her in the beach town of Montesilvano, Abruzzo, we sat on her balcony and enjoyed drinks and a selection of appetizers she had prepared. Among them were these dischi volanti *(flying saucers), small batter-fried eggplant sandwiches with the eggplant taking the place of bread. They were whimsical and delicious. The filling can be anything you like, but* prosciutto cotto, *mortadella, or salami and some sort of cheese are typical.*

EGGPLANT

1⅔ cups (210 g) unbleached all-purpose flour, plus more as needed

2 teaspoons baking powder

2 large eggs

¾ cup plus 2 tablespoons (200 ml) whole milk, plus more as needed

Fine sea salt

Pinch of freshly ground black pepper

Pinch of freshly grated nutmeg

2 smallish eggplants (not too wide), about ¾ lb (340 g) total weight

Sunflower or other neutral oil, for frying

FILLING

½ lb (225 g) thinly sliced prosciutto cotto (cooked Parma ham)

2 balls (½ lb/225 g each) milky fresh mozzarella cheese, thinly sliced

1 tablespoon minced fresh rosemary

MAKES ABOUT 12 SANDWICHES; 6–12 SERVINGS

To prepare the eggplant, in a bowl, whisk together the flour and baking powder. Make a well in the center and crack the eggs into the well. Slowly pour in the milk while stirring constantly with a fork or a whisk to mix together all the ingredients and work out any lumps. Once the batter is smooth, add ½ teaspoon salt, the pepper, and nutmeg and mix well. The batter should be slightly thicker than pancake batter. If the batter is too thick or thin, add more milk or flour as needed. Set aside.

Trim both ends off the eggplants and cut crosswise into slices ¼ inch (6 mm) thick. You should have about 24 slices.

Line a large plate with paper towels and set it near the stove. Pour the oil to a depth of 1½ inches (4 cm) into a deep frying pan or a heavy-bottomed saucepan and heat over medium-high heat to 325°–350°F (165°–180°C) on a deep-frying thermometer. (Or use the nonna trick: insert the handle of an unvarnished wooden spoon into the oil, and if the oil bubbles steadily around the handle, it is hot enough.) Working in batches, dip an eggplant slice into the batter, letting the excess drip off, and gently add it to the oil. Add as many dipped slices as will fit comfortably in the pan without crowding. Fry, turning once, until golden brown on both sides, 1–2 minutes on each side. Use a skimmer or tongs to transfer the slices to the towel-lined plate and sprinkle lightly with salt. Continue to batter and fry the eggplant slices until all the slices are fried.

To fill the sandwiches, layer the prosciutto cotto, mozzarella, and a sprinkle of rosemary on half of the fried eggplant slices, dividing the ingredients evenly, then top with a second eggplant slice. Secure each sandwich with a toothpick and arrange on a platter. Serve the sandwiches at room temperature, or zap them briefly in the microwave to serve them warm.

Giardiniera-Stuffed Eggs

There are a hundred ways to stuff a hard-boiled egg, from classic deviled to fillings enriched with bacon, crab, or caviar. These eggs stuffed with giardiniera *are my favorite. The Italian vegetable pickle adds just the right amount of crunch and vinegary punch to the creamy yolk filling without overwhelming it, and the colorful flecks make the eggs look pretty. It is worth the effort to force the cooked yolks through a sieve when you make the filling so they will blend to a creamy consistency ideal for mounding or piping into the egg white halves.*

6 extra-large eggs, at room temperature

½ cup (100 g) drained and finely chopped giardiniera

2 tablespoons mayonnaise, such as Duke's, Hellmann's, or Best Foods (not Miracle Whip)

¼ teaspoon fine sea salt

Freshly ground black pepper

Drained nonpareil capers, fresh flat-leaf parsley leaves, small pieces of jarred pimiento or roasted red pepper, giardiniera, or drained anchovy fillets in olive oil, for garnish

MAKES 12 STUFFED EGG HALVES; 6 SERVINGS

COOK'S NOTE
If not serving the stuffed eggs right away, cover with plastic wrap and refrigerate; I prefer them served somewhat chilled. They will keep in the refrigerator for up to 6 hours; let stand at room temperature for 15 minutes before serving.

Fit a saucepan with a steamer basket and add water to the pan to reach just below the bottom of the basket. Bring to a boil over medium-high heat. Carefully place the eggs in the basket and cover the pan with a lid. Set a timer for 15 minutes.

While the eggs are steaming, fill a bowl with cold water and add a handful of ice cubes. When the timer dings, turn off the heat and use a slotted spoon to transfer the eggs to the ice water. Let the eggs cool for a few minutes, then drain off the water. Gently crack each egg just enough to create little fractures in the shell and then peel. The shell should come off easily.

Set a fine-mesh sieve over a bowl. Cut each egg in half lengthwise with a sharp knife, rinsing or wiping the blade after each cut. Gently pop out the yolks into the sieve and use the back of a teaspoon to force them through the sieve into a bowl. Set the whites, hollow side up, on a platter or on an egg plate if you have one. If any of the egg white halves are rocking, slice a thin slice off the bottom so they hold steady.

Add the giardiniera and mayonnaise to the yolks and season with the salt and a grinding or two of pepper. Fold everything together until thoroughly mixed and creamy. Use a small coffee spoon to fill each egg white cavity with the yolk mixture, dividing it evenly and mounding it neatly. Alternatively, fit a pastry bag with a star tip or a plain wide tip and pipe the yolk mixture into the egg whites. Garnish each stuffed egg as you like and serve.

Zucchini Fritters with Fresh Herbs and Ricotta Salata

A plate of these savory three-bite fritters, tender and fragrant with herbs, along with a tomato and mozzarella salad, is, to my mind, the ideal summer supper. But they are meant to be an appetizer, and they are good at that too. The plate empties quickly whenever I serve them at parties.

1 large or 2 medium zucchini, about ½ lb (225 g) total weight

Fine sea salt

1 cup (125 g) unbleached all-purpose flour

¾ cup (180 ml) sparkling water

1 large egg

⅓–½ cup (90–100 g) crumbled ricotta salata

1 tablespoon finely chopped mixed fresh herbs, such as basil, dill, mint, and flat-leaf parsley

Sunflower oil or equal parts sunflower and extra-virgin olive oil, for frying

MAKES ABOUT 24 FRITTERS; 12 SERVINGS

Cut the zucchini lengthwise into quarters, then thinly slice the quarters crosswise. Transfer to a colander set over a bowl, sprinkle with salt, and toss to coat evenly. Let stand while you prepare the batter.

In a bowl, whisk together the flour and ½ teaspoon salt. Slowly pour in the water while whisking constantly to prevent lumps from forming. Crack the egg into the bowl and whisk until everything is well blended. The mixture should have the consistency of pancake batter and should fall in a ribbon when you lift some with the whisk. If the batter is too thick, add water, a few drops at a time, until the consistency is good.

Pat the zucchini dry and add it to the batter. Stir in the ricotta salata and herbs.

Line a large plate with paper towels and set it near the stove. Pour the oil to a depth of ¼ inch (6 mm) into a deep frying pan and heat over medium-high heat until it shimmers. The oil is ready when a small bead of batter dropped into it sizzles and immediately floats to the surface. Working in batches, gently drop spoonfuls (about 2 tablespoons) of the batter into the hot oil, taking care not to crowd the pan. Fry until golden brown on the bottom, 1–2 minutes. Using a fork, turn and fry on the other side until golden brown, 1–2 minutes longer. Use the fork or a skimmer to transfer the fritters to the towel-lined plate. Repeat until all the batter is fried.

Arrange the warm fritters on a platter, sprinkle lightly with salt, and serve.

Crostini Three Ways

Crostini (toasts) were once a traditional antipasto, garnished with such savory toppings as sautéed chicken livers, porcini mushrooms, or butter and anchovy. These days, the toppings are limited only by your own taste and imagination. Here are three of my favorites.

CROSTINI

1 slender baguette, cut on the diagonal into slices about ½ inch (12 mm) thick (20–24 slices)

Extra-virgin olive oil

EACH VARIATION MAKES
20–24 CROSTINI

To make the crostini, preheat the oven to 400°F (200°C). Arrange the baguette slices in a single layer on a large sheet pan and brush the tops lightly with the oil. Bake until the edges are lightly browned and the tops are golden, 8–10 minutes. Set aside to cool.

Crostini with Rapini and Stracciatella

2 cloves garlic, sliced paper-thin

¼ cup (60 ml) extra-virgin olive oil, plus more for finishing

1 small fresh chile, minced, or generous pinch of red pepper flakes

2 bunches rapini (broccoli rabe), about 1 lb (450 g) total weight, tough stems discarded and leaves and tender stems chopped

½ teaspoon fine sea salt

1 batch crostini

½ lb (225 g) stracciatella cheese

Put the garlic and oil into a large frying pan and set over medium-low heat. Cook, stirring once or twice, until the garlic is softened but not browned, about 7 minutes. Stir in the chile. Add the rapini by the handful, using tongs or a wooden spoon to toss and coat the greens with oil.

Cover and cook until the greens are wilted, about 2 minutes. Uncover, season with the salt, and toss once more. Re-cover and continue to cook at a gentle simmer until tender, 20–30 minutes. Uncover, raise the heat to medium, and cook until most of the liquid has evaporated, about 10 minutes more. Remove from the heat and let cool slightly.

Arrange the crostini on a platter and spoon the rapini on top, dividing it evenly. Dollop a small spoonful of stracciatella on each crostino and finish with a thread of oil.

Crostini with Anchovies and Olive Oil Butter

4 tablespoons (60 g) unsalted butter, at cool room temperature

2 tablespoons extra-virgin olive oil

Pinch of flaky sea salt

1 batch crostini

12–24 anchovy fillets in olive oil

In a small bowl, stir together the butter and oil until the oil is completely incorporated into the butter. Stir in the salt. Spread the butter mixture onto the crostini, dividing it evenly. Top each crostino with a piece of anchovy, using either half of a fillet or a whole one, depending on how much you love anchovies (I use whole ones). Arrange the crostini on a platter and serve.

Crostini with Marinated Tomatoes and Mozzarella

4 cups (680 g) cherry tomatoes (1½ lb), preferably a mix of varieties and colors, quartered

¼ cup (60 ml) extra-virgin olive oil

1 tablespoon red wine vinegar

¼ teaspoon fine sea salt

1 small handful fresh basil leaves (about 30 leaves)

1 ball (½ lb/225 g) milky fresh mozzarella cheese

1 batch crostini

1 tablespoon aged balsamic vinegar

Flaky sea salt

In a bowl, toss the tomatoes with the oil, red wine vinegar, and fine salt. Set aside to marinate for 30 minutes. Tear 4–5 basil leaves into pieces and stir them into the tomatoes. Reserve the remaining whole basil leaves for garnish.

Thinly slice the mozzarella. If necessary, cut the slices in half so they will fit neatly on top of the crostini.

Arrange the crostini on a platter. Lay the mozzarella on top and then spoon on the marinated tomatoes, dividing them evenly. Top each crostino with a thread of balsamic vinegar, a sprinkle of flaky salt, and a basil leaf, and serve.

Crostini Three Ways, page 20

Turin-Style Breadsticks with Prosciutto, page 24

Turin-Style Breadsticks with Prosciutto

Turin is famous for its extra-long grissini—aka breadsticks—with lots of snap and flavor. At some bakeries in and around the city, the crunchy sticks are as long as the arm span of the bakers who shape them. Grissini are easy to make. Simply stretch the lengths of dough as you transfer them to the sheet pan. Try them plain or flavor the dough with Parmigiano cheese and rosemary (see Cook's Note).

2 cups (250 g) unbleached all-purpose flour

2 cups (250 g) bread flour

1½ teaspoons instant yeast (not rapid-rise)

1½ teaspoons fine sea salt

1¼ cups (300 ml) warm water (105°–110°F/41°–43°C)

1 tablespoon pure maple syrup

2 tablespoons extra-virgin olive oil, plus more for brushing

Semolina flour, for dusting

Thin slices prosciutto di Parma (not trimmed of fat), at room temperature, for serving (optional)

MAKES 40–48 BREADSTICKS

Measure the all-purpose and bread flours, yeast, and salt into the bowl of a stand mixer fitted with the paddle attachment. Mix briefly on low speed to combine. Add the water, maple syrup, and oil and mix on low speed until the dough comes together. Switch to the dough hook and knead on medium speed until the dough is smooth and elastic, about 3 minutes. Or turn the dough out onto a clean work surface and knead by hand until smooth and elastic, about 6 minutes.

Lightly dust the work surface with semolina flour. Gently roll out the dough into an oval or rectangle about 6 inches (15 cm) wide and 12–14 inches (30–35 cm) long. Brush the surface lightly with oil and then dust lightly with semolina flour. Cover the dough with plastic wrap and let sit until about doubled in size, about 2 hours. It will be nicely puffed.

About 20 minutes before the dough has finished rising, preheat the oven to 450°F (230°C). Line two 11 x 17-inch (28 x 43-cm) sheet pans with parchment paper.

Using a knife with a long, sharp blade, cut a strip of dough about ⅜ inch (1 cm) wide from the short end of the puffed slab. Carefully grasp an end of the strip in each hand and pull the strip gently, stretching it to fit the length of a prepared sheet pan. Lay the strip on the pan. Cut and shape several more, adding them to the sheet pan and spacing them about 1 inch (2.5 cm) apart. You should be able to fit 7 or 8 strips.

Slip the pan into the oven and bake the grissini until golden brown, 10–12 minutes. Keep an eye on them during the last couple of minutes to prevent overbaking. Transfer the grissini to a wire rack and let cool completely. While the first batch is baking, ready another batch on the second sheet pan and slip it into the oven as soon as the first batch emerges. Repeat until all the dough is shaped and baked.

Store the cooled grissini in a large airtight container, such as a lidded plastic container, or in an airtight plastic bread storage bag (available at gourmet shops and online). They will keep at room temperature for up to 2 weeks.

The grissini are quite long (up to 17 inches/43 cm). To serve with prosciutto, snap them in half and roll a thin slice of prosciutto around each half. Make as many as you like, depending on the number of people you are serving. Arrange the wrapped grissini on a platter and serve.

COOK'S NOTE
To flavor the grissini with Parmigiano and rosemary, add 1 cup (115 g) freshly grated Parmigiano Reggiano cheese and 2 tablespoons minced fresh rosemary to the dry ingredients and proceed as directed.

Italian Sour

My husband, Scott, is an Italian wine and drinks aficionado. This cocktail is his clever riff on the New York sour. The original is made with bourbon, lemon juice, simple syrup, and red wine. The most eye-catching feature of the drink is the red wine "float," which contributes an appealing complexity and a pretty two-toned appearance. To make this drink distinctly Italian, Scott swapped out the bourbon for semisweet vermouth bianco and chose Nero d'Avola, a robust Sicilian red, for the wine topper.

Ice cubes

1 lemon

2 fl oz (60 ml) vermouth bianco, such as Poli Gran Bassano, Contratto, or Martini & Rossi, or French vermouth blanc (see Bartender's Note)

½ fl oz (15 ml) Basic Simple Syrup (see below)

1 fl oz (30 ml) Nero d'Avola or other robust red wine

MAKES 1 COCKTAIL

Fill a cocktail shaker or pitcher one-third full with ice. Partially fill a highball glass with ice. Remove a long strip of peel from the lemon and drop it into the glass. Then squeeze 1 fl oz (30 ml) juice from the lemon.

Pour the vermouth into the shaker, followed by the lemon juice and simple syrup. Using a bar spoon or other long-handled spoon, stir vigorously for 15 seconds. Strain into the highball glass.

Position the spoon with the back (convex) side facing up over the glass, tilting it down at a 45-degree angle. Slowly pour the wine over the back of the spoon into the glass; the wine will float on top. Serve at once.

BASIC SIMPLE SYRUP
To make simple syrup, in a small saucepan, combine ¼ cup (50 g) sugar and ¼ cup (60 ml) water over low heat and heat, stirring constantly, until the sugar dissolves. Pour into a small heatproof jar and let cool completely before using. Store leftover simple syrup tightly capped in the refrigerator, where it will keep for up to 1 month.

BARTENDER'S NOTE
Vermouth bianco (Italian) or vermouth blanc (French) is a slightly sweetened version of dry vermouth. If you can't find either one, substitute a good-quality vermouth that is labeled "dry" and use 1 fl oz (30 ml) simple syrup in the cocktail. It is best to avoid vermouth labeled "extra dry" for this drink.

Bitter Lemon Vinegroni

This fresh twist on the ever-popular Negroni comes from Sarah Conezio and Isaiah Billington, two pastry chefs turned vinegar makers. Their Pennsylvania-based company, Keepwell Vinegar, makes a range of artisanal vinegars, miso pastes, and fermented sauces. Their bitter lemon vinegar is made from the small wild, pithy, and seedy lemons that thrive, unexpectedly, in the mid-Atlantic region. You can substitute a good-quality small-batch cider vinegar or artisanal white wine vinegar.

Ice cubes

1 fl oz (30 ml) gin

1 fl oz (30 ml) sweet vermouth

½ fl oz (15 ml) bitter lemon vinegar or small-batch cider vinegar

1 orange or bitter lemon (if you can find it) twist, for garnish

MAKES 1 COCKTAIL

Fill a cocktail shaker half full with ice. Pour the gin into the shaker, followed by the vermouth and vinegar. Using a bar spoon or other long-handled spoon, stir vigorously for 15 seconds. Strain into a small tumbler, garnish with the twist, and serve.

Rome with a View

Bartender Michael McIlroy, based in New York City and Nashville, created this citrus-spiked cocktail starring Campari, dry vermouth, and fresh lime juice. It's just the sort of drink you want to be sipping while seated at a small table in a half-hidden piazza, reading a book and watching the late-summer sun move across the sky.

Ice cubes

1 fl oz (30 ml) Campari

1 fl oz (30 ml) dry vermouth

1 fl oz (30 ml) fresh lime juice

¾ fl oz (20 ml) Basic Simple Syrup (page 26)

Soda water, for topping off

1 orange wheel, for garnish

MAKES 1 COCKTAIL

Fill a cocktail shaker half full with ice. Fill a collins (tall) glass with ice.

Pour the Campari into the shaker, followed by the vermouth, lime juice, and simple syrup. Cover and shake vigorously until chilled. Strain into the collins glass and top off with the soda water. Garnish with the orange wheel and serve.

Garibaldi Spritz

A spritz cocktail is the perfect way to take the edge off a sweltering summer afternoon. This one is named for nineteenth-century revolutionary Giuseppe Garibaldi, who led the unification of Italy. It combines Campari, which originated in Lombardy, with oranges, which grow abundantly in Sicily. Prosecco gives it the fizz. Find a table in the shade, tip back your glass, and enjoy.

Ice cubes

1½ fl oz (45 ml) Campari

3½ fl oz (105 ml) fresh orange juice

Prosecco, for topping off

1 orange wheel, for garnish

MAKES 1 COCKTAIL

Fill a collins glass with ice. Pour in the Campari and orange juice and stir. Top off with the Prosecco, garnish with the orange wheel, and serve.

SOUP
—
SALAD

Pasta and White Bean Soup with Delicata Squash

One afternoon years ago, my husband and I came upon a colorful eatery in the Flaminia neighborhood of Rome. It was well past lunch, but the place was still serving, so we went in for a bowl of the soup of the day, a nourishing mix of beans, pumpkin, and kale. I've made it often since then, sometimes with different beans, sometimes without kale. In this version, I've added pasta, for a one-bowl meal. Garnish each serving with a generous drizzle of olive oil.

¼ cup (60 ml) extra-virgin olive oil, plus more for serving

1 piece pancetta, about 1 oz (30 g)

1 yellow onion, chopped

1 large carrot, peeled and diced

2 celery ribs, diced

1 clove garlic, lightly crushed

1 small fresh red chile, minced, or pinch of red pepper flakes

2 tablespoons finely chopped fresh herbs, such as flat-leaf parsley, rosemary, and sage

Fine sea salt

1 bunch dinosaur (Tuscan) kale, about ½ lb (225 g), tough stems removed, leaves chopped

1 delicata squash, about 1 lb (450 g), peeled, seeded, and cubed to yield 3 cups (400 g)

4–6 cups (950 ml–1.4 l) vegetable broth, chicken broth, or water

2 cups (340 g) cannellini or borlotti beans with liquid, home-cooked (see page 34) or canned

1 cup (240 g) tomato passata (purée)

2-inch (5-cm) piece Parmigiano Reggiano cheese rind, plus freshly grated cheese for serving

1–1½ cups (100–150 g) small pasta, such as shells or tubetti

MAKES 4–6 SERVINGS

Pour the oil into a heavy-bottomed pot. Add the pancetta, then tip in the onion, carrot, and celery and set over medium heat. Stir in the garlic, chile, and herbs and cook, stirring often, until the vegetables have softened, 8–10 minutes. Stir in 1 teaspoon salt.

Add the kale by the handful, stirring it into the vegetables and allowing it to wilt as you go. When all of the kale has been added, tip in the squash and about 1 cup (240 ml) of the broth. Cover and cook at a gentle simmer until the squash begins to soften and the kale is well on its way to tenderness, 15–20 minutes.

Stir in the beans and their liquid. Pour in the tomato passata and simmer, uncovered, for 5 minutes. Add 3 cups (700 ml) of the broth and toss in the Parmigiano rind, then raise the heat to medium-high and bring to a boil. Reduce the heat to medium and cook until the squash is tender, another 10 minutes or so. Use the back of a spoon to mash some of the squash cubes and beans against the side of the pot; this will give the soup a dense, creamy texture. If the soup is too thick, add another 1–2 cups (240–475 ml) broth to thin as needed and bring to a boil over medium-high heat. Tip in the pasta and stir to prevent it from sticking. Reduce the heat to medium-low and let the soup simmer until the pasta is cooked, 10–15 minutes. The cooking time will depend on the size and shape of the pasta. Keep in mind that pasta in soup tends to take longer to cook than pasta in boiling water. If the soup seems too thick as the pasta is cooking, add more liquid.

When the pasta is cooked, remove and discard the cheese rind. Ladle the soup into bowls, top with a drizzle of oil and a shower of Parmigiano, and serve.

Chickpea and Celery Soup with Farro

While I love minestrone chock-full of colorful vegetables, I also love a pared-down soup that showcases one or two ingredients. Here the stars are celery and chickpeas. Look for freshly harvested bunches of celery with their leaves still attached at fall farmers' markets. As for the chickpeas, in a pinch you can use canned, but cooking them yourself is easy, they taste much better, and you can add their savory cooking liquid to your soup.

2-oz (60-g) piece pancetta, diced

4 tablespoons (60 ml) extra-virgin olive oil, plus more for serving

1 small yellow onion, halved and thinly sliced

1 celery heart (the center stalks from a bunch) or 3 large ribs with leaves, diced

1 clove garlic, lightly crushed

1 tablespoon minced fresh rosemary

Pinch of red pepper flakes

2 cups (340 g) chickpeas with liquid, home-cooked or canned

2 cups (475 ml) chicken or vegetable broth, preferably homemade (see page 38)

2 cups (475 ml) water

1 cup (180 g) pearled farro, rinsed

Generous pinch of fine sea salt

Freshly grated Parmigiano Reggiano cheese, for serving

MAKES 4–6 SERVINGS

In a heavy-bottomed pot over medium heat, combine the pancetta and 2 tablespoons of the oil and cook, stirring often, until the pancetta is lightly crisped, about 10 minutes. Stir in the onion, celery, garlic, and the remaining 2 tablespoons oil and cook, stirring from time to time, until the onion and celery are softened, about 10 minutes. Stir in the rosemary and red pepper flakes, followed by the chickpeas and 1 cup (240 ml) of their cooking water if using home-cooked beans or the liquid from the can plus enough water to make 1 cup (240 ml) if using canned beans. Bring to a simmer and cook until most of the liquid is absorbed, about 5 minutes.

Pour in the broth and water, bring to a simmer, and cook, partially covered, until the celery is very tender and the soup has thickened, 20–30 minutes.

While the soup is simmering, cook the farro. In a saucepan, combine the farro with water to cover by 2 inches (5 cm) and the salt. Bring to a boil over medium-high heat and skim off any foam from the surface. Reduce the heat to a simmer and cook just until tender but still a bit chewy, 20–30 minutes.

When the celery is tender, use a potato masher to mash up about one-third of the celery and chickpeas. Spoon the farro directly into the soup and simmer, partially covered, until the grains are fully tender and the soup is nicely thickened, about 20 minutes. Remove from the heat, cover, and let sit for 10 minutes before serving. (The soup can sit, covered, for a couple of hours before reheating and serving. Or it can be cooled and refrigerated overnight and then reheated the next day.)

Ladle the soup into bowls, top each bowl with a drizzle of oil and a shower of Parmigiano, and serve.

Summer Minestrone Two Ways

This is my go-to summer minestrone—packed with vegetables and served at room temperature rather than hot. This recipe makes a lot of soup, so once it's cooked, I usually set aside half of it to purée with a few splashes of cream, which I then refrigerate until well chilled. The result is a delicious cream of vegetable soup, perfect for a humid summer afternoon or evening.

SOUP

Rounded 1 cup (225 g) dried cannellini or Great Northern beans, soaked overnight in cold water to cover

1 clove garlic, lightly crushed

2 fresh sage sprigs

1 white onion, diced

1 celery heart (the center stalks from a bunch) or 3 large ribs with leaves, diced

3 carrots, peeled and diced

1 yellow potato, peeled and cut into ½-inch (12-mm) cubes

2 leeks, white and pale green parts, thinly sliced

2 zucchini, cut into ½-inch (12-mm) pieces

2 cups (280 g) frozen peas, thawed

½ lb (225 g) green beans, trimmed and cut into ½-inch (12-mm) pieces

2 cups (340 g) fresh corn kernels (from 3–4 ears)

Fine sea salt and freshly ground black pepper

To make the soup, drain and rinse the cannellini beans. Put them in a Dutch oven or heavy-bottomed saucepan with fresh water to cover by 2 inches (5 cm). Add the garlic and 1 sage sprig and bring to a boil over medium-high heat, skimming off any foam that forms on the surface. Reduce the heat to medium and cook, uncovered, at a gentle simmer until tender, about 1 hour, depending on the type and age of the beans. Remove from the heat, cover, and let rest.

In a large pot, combine the onion, celery, carrots, potato, leeks, zucchini, peas, green beans, and corn. Pour in water, stopping when the vegetables are not quite covered, then stir in 1 tablespoon salt and add the remaining sage sprig. Bring to a boil over medium-high heat, reduce the heat to medium, and simmer gently, uncovered, until the carrots and potato are tender, 15–20 minutes.

Using a slotted spoon, scoop the cooked cannellini beans into the soup. You can add some of the bean liquid as well, if you like. Season with pepper and with more salt if needed and cook for 5–10 minutes to blend the flavors. Remove from the heat, remove and discard the sage, and let the soup cool to room temperature while you make the pesto.

BASIL PESTO

2 handfuls fresh basil leaves

1 handful fresh flat-leaf parsley leaves

2 small cloves garlic, coarsely chopped

3 tablespoons pine nuts

½ teaspoon coarse sea salt

About ½ cup (120 ml) extra-virgin olive oil

½ cup (60 g) freshly grated Parmigiano Reggiano cheese

FOR SERVING

Extra-virgin olive oil

Freshly grated Parmigiano Reggiano cheese

MAKES 6–8 SERVINGS

To make the pesto, in a food processor, combine the basil, parsley, garlic, pine nuts, and salt and pulse to chop the herbs. With the motor running, drizzle in enough oil to make a soft, spoonable paste. Scrape the pesto into a bowl and stir in the cheese. (If not using immediately, cover with plastic wrap, pressing the wrap directly onto the surface of the pesto to prevent browning.)

Ladle the soup into bowls. Top each bowl with a spoonful of pesto, a drizzle of oil, and some grated cheese, and serve.

To make the cream of vegetable soup, using a high-powered blender or immersion blender, purée whatever is left over until smooth. Add some heavy cream, vegetable broth, or water—anywhere from ½–1 cup (120–240 ml), depending on how thick the purée is—to give it the proper consistency. Transfer to a container with a tight-fitting lid and refrigerate until well chilled (up to overnight). Serve cold, topped with a dollop of the pesto.

Summer Minestrone Two Ways, page 34

Crepe "Noodles" in Homemade Broth, page 38

Crepe "Noodles" in Homemade Broth

Delicate crepes, rolled up and cut into ribbons, take the place of pasta in this nourishing soup. You'll need homemade broth to do it justice, so start this recipe the day before you plan to serve it and be sure to use a high-quality bird.

CHICKEN BROTH

1 whole organic chicken, 4–4½ lb (1.8–2 kg)

4 whole cloves

2 yellow onions, quartered

3 carrots, peeled and cut into 2-inch (5-cm) pieces

2 celery ribs with leafy tops, cut into 2-inch (5-cm) pieces

6 fresh flat-leaf parsley sprigs

4 fresh thyme sprigs

½ teaspoon black peppercorns

About 4 qt (3.8 l) water

Fine sea salt

CREPE "NOODLES"

¾ cup (95 g) unbleached all-purpose flour, sifted

4 large eggs, lightly beaten

2 cups (475 ml) low-fat milk

2 tablespoons finely chopped fresh flat-leaf parsley

½ teaspoon fine sea salt

Pinch of freshly grated nutmeg

1–2 tablespoons unsalted butter

Freshly grated Parmigiano Reggiano cheese, for serving

MAKES 4 SERVINGS

To make the broth, place the chicken in a large stockpot. Stick 1 clove into each of 4 of the onion quarters, then add the 4 onion quarters to the pot along with the remaining onion quarters and the carrots, celery, parsley, thyme, and peppercorns. Add the water to cover all the ingredients by about 2 inches (5 cm) and bring to a boil over medium-high heat, skimming off any foam that forms on the surface. Reduce the heat to low and simmer gently, uncovered, until the liquid is reduced by about half, 3–4 hours. Season with salt during the last 30 minutes of cooking.

Lift the chicken from the pot and transfer it to a large bowl. Let cool until it can be handled, then remove and discard the skin and bones. Reserve the meat for another use (I like to drizzle it with olive oil and sprinkle it with salt and pepper and serve it warm as a second course). Use a spider or large slotted spoon to remove the vegetables from the pot. Discard the vegetables.

Line a colander with damp cheesecloth and place it over a large bowl. Strain the broth into the bowl and let cool to room temperature. Transfer the broth to a covered container and refrigerate until thoroughly chilled. Skim off and discard the congealed layer of fat on the surface. Measure out 6 cups (1.4 l) broth for the soup. Refrigerate or freeze the remaining broth for another use.

To make the crepe "noodles," in a blender, combine the flour, eggs, milk, parsley, salt, and nutmeg and blend until smooth. Transfer the batter to a bowl, cover, and let rest at room temperature for 30 minutes.

Place a 9-inch (23-cm) nonstick frying pan over medium heat and melt just enough of the butter to film the bottom. When the pan is hot, add a ladleful of batter—about ¼ cup (60 ml)—to the center of the pan and quickly swirl and tilt the pan so the batter evenly and completely coats the bottom, forming a thin pancake. Cook just until the top is set, 30–45 seconds. Flip the crepe and cook until the underside is lightly golden, 20–30 seconds, then transfer the crepe to a plate. Continue until you have used all the batter, making sure to butter the pan lightly from time to time to prevent sticking and stacking the crepes as they are cooked. You should end up with 12 crepes.

Roll up each crepe cigar-style and cut crosswise into thin ¼–½ inch (6–12 mm) ribbons. These are your "noodles."

Pour the 6 cups (1.4 l) broth into a saucepan and bring to a boil over medium heat. When the broth is boiling, drop in the crepe "noodles" and cook just until warmed through. Ladle the broth and "noodles" into shallow rimmed bowls, top each bowl with a shower of Parmigiano, and serve.

COOK'S NOTE
Both the crepes and broth can be made in advance. Layer waxed or parchment paper between the crepes and slip the stack into a lock-top plastic bag or an airtight container. Pour the broth into a tightly capped jar or similar airtight container. Store the crepes and broth in the refrigerator for up to 3 days or in the freezer for up to 1 month.

Zucchini and Potato Summer Potage

Zucchini, potato, and leeks form a flavorful trio for a light, summery dish. The nice thing about a simple soup like this is that you can prep the ingredients as you go, bringing a relaxed rhythm to the cooking process.

3 leeks, white and pale green parts, thinly sliced

¼ cup (60 ml) extra-virgin olive oil, plus more for drizzling

2 yellow potatoes, about 1 lb (450 g) total weight

3 zucchini, about 1 lb (450 g) total weight

2 tablespoons finely chopped fresh herbs, such as flat-leaf parsley, marjoram, and mint

1 teaspoon fine sea salt

4 cups (950 ml) water

2-inch (5-cm) piece Parmigiano Reggiano cheese rind

Freshly grated Parmigiano Reggiano cheese, for serving

MAKES 4 SERVINGS

In a heavy-bottomed saucepan over medium-low heat, combine the leeks and oil and cook, stirring every now and then, until the leeks have softened, about 7 minutes. While the leeks are cooking, peel the potatoes and cut them into ½-inch (12-mm) dice. Tip the potatoes into the pan, stir to coat with the oil, and cook, stirring every now and again. While the potatoes are cooking, cut the zucchini lengthwise into quarters, then cut crosswise into wedges about ¼ inch (6 mm) thick. Tip the zucchini into the pan and stir to mix well with the other ingredients. Add the herbs and salt and continue to cook, stirring often, until the vegetables are starting to become tender, 10–15 minutes.

Pour in the water, add the cheese rind, and raise the heat to medium-high. Bring to a boil, then reduce the heat to medium-low, cover partially, and simmer until all the vegetables are very tender, 35–45 minutes. Reduce the heat more if necessary to maintain a gentle simmer. As the soup cooks, using the back of a spoon, press some of the potatoes and zucchini against the side of the pan to mash them. This will help to thicken the soup and give it a creamy texture without puréeing it completely. The soup is done when it's nicely thickened and has a rich vegetable flavor. Remove and discard the cheese rind, then taste and adjust the seasoning with salt if needed.

Ladle the soup into bowls, top each bowl with a drizzle of oil and a shower of Parmigiano, and serve.

Cream of Carrot and Buttercup Squash Soup with Rosemary Oil

The Italian word for a creamed soup is vellutata, *which roughly translates to "turned to velvet," and that's exactly what takes place here. The carrots and squash are roasted to tenderness and then puréed with broth to velvety smoothness.*

ROSEMARY OIL

1 tablespoon fresh rosemary leaves

¼ cup (60 ml) extra-virgin olive oil

SOUP

1 buttercup squash, about 1½ lb (680 g), halved, seeded, peeled, and cut into chunks

1 lb (450 g) carrots, peeled and cut into chunks

2 yellow onions, cut into chunks

2 cloves garlic, coarsely chopped

4 fresh thyme sprigs

3–4 fresh flat-leaf parsley sprigs

1 teaspoon fine sea salt

Freshly ground black pepper

½ cup (120 ml) extra-virgin olive oil

4 cups (950 ml) chicken or vegetable broth, preferably homemade (see page 38), plus more as needed

6–8 fresh rosemary sprigs, for garnish

MAKES 6–8 SERVINGS

To make the rosemary oil, put the rosemary into a small, heavy-bottomed saucepan and cover with the oil. Set over low heat and heat until the oil is warmed through, 5–10 minutes. The oil should not reach a simmer. Remove from the heat and let steep for 1 hour while you make the soup.

To make the soup, preheat the oven to 425°F (220°C). Combine the squash, carrots, onions, garlic, thyme, and parsley in a roasting pan and season with the salt and several grindings of pepper. Drizzle the oil over the vegetables and toss to coat. Roast, stirring every 15 minutes, until tender and browned in spots, 30–45 minutes.

Remove and discard the thyme and parsley sprigs. Transfer the vegetables to a Dutch oven or other heavy-bottomed pot and pour in the broth. Purée the soup with an immersion blender until smooth. Or use a blender to purée the soup in two batches and transfer to the pot. Add more broth to thin the soup to the desired consistency. Place over medium-low heat and cook, stirring a few times, until warmed through, about 10 minutes.

Strain the rosemary-infused oil through a fine-mesh sieve into a small pitcher.

Ladle the soup into bowls and drizzle the top of each bowl with a little of the rosemary oil. Garnish each bowl with a rosemary sprig and serve.

Peaches and Tomatoes with Fresh Mint, Basil, and Burrata

There is nothing prettier than the rosy blush of summer peaches, except maybe this salad, which combines them with garden-fresh tomatoes and creamy burrata cheese. For a refreshing starter—or even a savory end to a light meal—serve with grilled bread to soak up the juices.

2 large ripe peaches, halved, pitted, and thinly sliced

3 tomatoes, preferably a mix of varieties and colors, thinly sliced

1 ball (½ lb/225 g) burrata cheese, at room temperature

1 tablespoon fruity red wine vinegar

2–3 tablespoons extra-virgin olive oil

1 handful small fresh mint and basil leaves, preferably a mix of green and purple basil

Flaky sea salt

MAKES 4 SERVINGS

Arrange the peaches and tomatoes on a platter.

Slice open the burrata and transfer the creamy filling to a bowl. Chop the "skin" of the burrata, add to the filling, and stir to mix. Dollop the burrata on top of the peaches and tomatoes.

In a small bowl, whisk together the vinegar and 2 tablespoons of the oil until emulsified to make a dressing. Taste and adjust with more oil if needed. Drizzle the dressing evenly over the salad. Sprinkle the mint and basil on top, followed by a generous pinch of salt, then serve.

Mushroom-Fennel Carpaccio with Shaved Parmigiano and Gremolata

It may sound odd, but I like to serve this at Thanksgiving. Brightly flavored with parsley and lemon, it's the perfect counterpoint to all the rich foods that dominate our national holiday. What's more, it requires no cooking, so it doesn't take up prime real estate on the stove or in the oven. Use your best olive oil, preferably olio nuovo, *and the highest-grade Parmigiano Reggiano cheese to make this simple dish shine.*

GREMOLATA

½ cup (15 g) fresh flat-leaf parsley leaves

1 small clove garlic

Zest of 1 small lemon, in strips

2 tablespoons fresh lemon juice

½ teaspoon fine sea salt

4–5 tablespoons (60–75 ml) extra-virgin olive oil

6 large cremini mushrooms, 2 ½–3 inches (6–7.5 cm) in diameter, about ½ lb (225 g) total weight, brushed clean

1 small fennel bulb

1 handful baby arugula

¼ cup (20 g) shaved Parmigiano Reggiano cheese

MAKES 4 SERVINGS

To make the gremolata, chop together the parsley, garlic, and lemon zest until you have a fine mince. Set aside in a small bowl.

In a separate small bowl, whisk together the lemon juice, salt, and 4 tablespoons (60 ml) of the oil until emulsified to make a dressing. Taste and adjust with more oil if needed.

Trim the stem end of each mushroom, then cut the mushrooms top to bottom into very thin slices. Cut off the stems and feathery tops from the fennel bulb; reserve the stems for another use and the tops for the garnish. Cut the bulb lengthwise into quarters and trim away the hard core. Slice the quarters lengthwise into very thin wedges.

Spread the arugula on a large platter. Arrange the mushroom slices and fennel wedges on top of the arugula, overlapping them slightly. Drizzle the dressing over the mushrooms and sprinkle the gremolata on top. Scatter the Parmigiano and reserved fennel tops over everything.

Let sit at room temperature for 15–30 minutes before serving (no longer, as the mushrooms will begin to release liquid).

Red Endive with Anchovy Dressing

Torpedo-shaped red Belgian endive, with its creamy white leaves and deep burgundy tips, makes a dramatic-looking and delicious salad. Think of the endive as a gentler version of radicchio—crunchy and fresh but more tender and less bitter, and a great match for a walnut-enriched anchovy dressing.

4 heads red Belgian endive

1 handful ice cubes

1 clove garlic

Generous pinch of coarse sea salt

3 tablespoons walnut pieces

4 anchovy fillets in olive oil, drained

1 tablespoon white or red wine vinegar

4–5 tablespoons (60–75 ml) extra-virgin olive oil

MAKES 4 SERVINGS

Separate each endive head into leaves, cutting away the heart as you go to dislodge the leaves. You can either discard the pieces of heart or thinly slice them and add them to the salad. Rinse the leaves. Fill a large bowl with cold water, add the ice, and immerse the endive in the ice water.

Cut the garlic clove in half lengthwise, and if there is a green heart, remove and discard it (it can be bitter). In a mortar with a pestle, pound together the garlic and salt, breaking up the garlic. Add the walnuts and pound to a coarse paste, then pound in the anchovies. Drizzle in the vinegar and use the pestle or a spoon to mix it into the paste. Drizzle in 4 tablespoons (60 ml) of the oil and stir until the dressing comes together. Taste and adjust with more oil if needed.

Drain the endive leaves and spin or pat them dry. Arrange the leaves in a serving bowl and spoon the dressing on top. Toss and serve.

Arugula with Fresh Figs, Blue Cheese, and Toasted Hazelnuts

I make this colorful salad whenever fresh figs are in season—generally in fall but sometimes in late summer. The recipe calls for Gorgonzola, a natural partner for figs, but use your favorite blue cheese. If fresh figs aren't available, you can substitute dried figs, but only if they are soft and plump.

¼ cup (60 ml) extra-virgin olive oil

2 tablespoons fig vinegar (see Cook's Note)

½ teaspoon fine sea salt

5 cups (100 g) arugula

2–3 oz (60–90 g) Gorgonzola piccante or other salty, pungent blue cheese, crumbled

6–8 ripe figs, stemmed and halved lengthwise

Freshly ground black pepper

¼ cup (28 g) toasted skinned hazelnuts, lightly crushed or chopped coarsley

MAKES 6 SERVINGS

To make a dressing, in a small bowl, whisk together the oil, vinegar, and salt until emulsified. Put the arugula into a bowl, drizzle with the dressing, and toss to coat evenly. Arrange the dressed greens on a platter.

Strew the cheese over the greens and arrange the figs on top. Finish with a grinding of pepper and serve.

COOK'S NOTE

Fig vinegar is available at specialty markets and online, but it is easy to make your own in just a few months. Put 1 cup (125 g) chopped dried Mission figs and 3 fresh lemon thyme sprigs in a heatproof jar with a lid. Bring 2 cups (475 ml) white wine vinegar to a simmer. Do not allow it to boil. Pour the hot vinegar over the figs and cap the jar. Let cool to room temperature, then set in a cool, dark spot to steep for 2–4 weeks. Line a fine-mesh sieve with damp cheesecloth and strain the vinegar. Using a funnel, transfer the vinegar to a bottle and cap it. Store in a cool, dark place in your pantry for at least 3 months before using. It will keep for up to 1 year. (If the vinegar develops mold or shows signs of fermentation, such as bubbles, cloudiness, or sliminess, discard it and sterilize the bottle before reusing it.)

Orange Salad with Radicchio, Red Onion, and Taggiasca Olives

Taggiasca olives are small and range from dark green to purple-black. They are grown in the western part of Liguria and are prized for their delicate earthy taste and for the buttery olive oil they produce. Similar to the Niçoise olives of the nearby French Riviera (which can be substituted), they pair especially well with the bright tang of citrus.

½ small red onion (about ¼ lb/60 g), thinly sliced

3 tablespoons white wine vinegar

1 tablespoon white or red balsamic vinegar

Pinch of fine sea salt

4 oranges in mixed varieties, such as navel, Cara Cara, and blood

6 large radicchio di Chioggia leaves (common round variety with burgundy leaves and white ribs)

16 Taggiasca olives

3 tablespoons extra-virgin olive oil, preferably Ligurian

Flaky sea salt and freshly ground black pepper

MAKES 4–6 SERVINGS

In a small bowl or container, toss the onion with both vinegars and the fine salt. (I like to put everything into a container with a lid so I can shake it up a bit.) Set aside to steep for 30 minutes.

Using a serrated knife, cut a thin slice off both ends of 1 orange, revealing the flesh. Stand the orange upright and, following the contour of the fruit, cut down to remove the peel and pith in wide strips, leaving beautiful orbs of naked orange flesh. Slice the orange into thin wheels. Repeat with the remaining 3 oranges.

To compose the salad, leave the radicchio leaves whole or cut them into narrow strips. Either way, distribute them evenly on a platter and top with the orange slices, overlapping them slightly. Drain the onion slices and scatter them here and there over the oranges. Arrange the olives on top of the onion slices. Drizzle the oil over the salad and season with a generous pinch of flaky salt and a few grindings of pepper.

Let the salad sit for a bit—no more than 5 minutes—before serving.

Aeolian Bread Salad

Named for the Greek demigod of winds, the Aeolian Islands are a collection of seven volcanic islands in the Tyrrhenian Sea between Sicily and the Italian peninsula. Composed of local ingredients, the cuisine of the islands is healthful and appetizing. This piquant salad of olives, capers, tomatoes, potatoes, and oil-packed tuna is a good example.

3 tablespoons capers, preferably salt-preserved

6 baby potatoes, about 6 oz (170 g) total weight, halved

5 tablespoons (75 ml) extra-virgin olive oil, plus more for drizzling

Fine sea salt and freshly ground black pepper

2 large, thick slices coarse country bread

1 clove garlic, lightly crushed

1 small head romaine lettuce, about ½ lb (225 g), cored and cut crosswise into strips 1 inch (2.5 cm) wide

1 large cucumber, peeled, halved lengthwise, seeded, and cut into bite-size pieces

1 medium or 2 small red torpedo onions, halved lengthwise and cut into paper-thin half-moons

1 cup (170 g) cherry tomatoes, halved

½ cup (70 g) pitted Gaeta or Kalamata olives

3 tablespoons red or white wine vinegar

1 can (5 oz/140 g) tuna in extra-virgin olive oil, drained

1 handful fresh basil leaves, torn

MAKES 4 SERVINGS

If using capers in salt, put them into a colander and rinse them well under running cold water. Transfer to a bowl, cover with cool water, and set aside to soak for 30 minutes. Drain and pat dry. If using capers in brine, rinse well under running cold water and pat dry.

Place the potatoes in a medium pot with water to cover by 2 inches (5 cm). Bring to a boil over medium-high heat and cook until tender, about 20 minutes. Drain in a colander set in the sink, then transfer to a bowl. Drizzle with 2 tablespoons of the oil and season with ½ teaspoon salt and a few grindings of pepper. Set aside to cool.

Turn the oven to broil and position the rack 4 inches (10 cm) from the element. Arrange the bread slices on a small sheet pan and broil until nicely browned and charred around the edges, 2–3 minutes. Remove from the oven and rub the top of each slice while still warm with the garlic clove. Cut or tear each slice into 1-inch (2.5-cm) pieces.

Put the lettuce into a large, shallow salad bowl. Scatter the cucumber, onion, and tomatoes on top of the lettuce. Add the cooled potatoes and the olives. Season with a generous pinch of salt and a few grindings of pepper. Dress with the remaining 3 tablespoons oil and the vinegar and toss to combine everything.

Separate the tuna into chunks and arrange the chunks on top of the salad. Sprinkle on the capers. Tuck in the bread pieces and scatter the basil leaves on top. Drizzle a little more oil on top and serve.

Roasted Beet Salad with Gorgonzola and Walnuts

Here is one of my favorite illustrations of the cooking adage, "What grows together goes together." Sweet beets, savory Gorgonzola, and buttery walnuts are all cultivated or produced in Lombardy and other parts of northern Italy, so it makes perfect sense that they would come together beautifully in this fall salad.

3 large beets, about ¾ lb (340 g) total weight

4 tablespoons (60 ml) extra-virgin olive oil

½ cup (60 g) walnut pieces

1 tablespoon red wine vinegar

½ teaspoon fine sea salt

¼ red onion, cut into thin wedges

2 oz (60 g) Gorgonzola dolce cheese, cut into pieces

MAKES 4 SERVINGS

Preheat the oven to 400°F (200°C).

Trim the stem and root end of each beet, then rub the beets with 1 tablespoon of the oil. Arrange the beets in a single layer on a sheet of aluminum foil, bring up the sides of the foil, and seal the edges securely closed to form a packet. Set the packet on a small sheet pan. Bake until tender, 45–50 minutes. They are ready if a cake tester or thin metal skewer inserted through the foil slides easily to the center of a beet. Remove from the oven and open the foil to let the beets cool until they can be handled.

Reduce the oven temperature to 350°F (180°C). Spread the walnuts on a small sheet pan or a pie pan and toast until they have taken on color and are fragrant, about 7 minutes. Pour them onto a cutting board, let cool, and chop coarsely.

When the beets are cool enough to handle, peel them and cut them lengthwise into quarters. Cut each quarter crosswise into small, fat wedges and transfer to a bowl.

To make a dressing, in a small bowl, whisk together the vinegar, salt, and remaining 3 tablespoons oil until emulsified.

Pour the dressing over the beets while they are still warm and toss to coat well. Add the onion and toss again. Let the salad sit for at least 1 hour or up to 3 hours to allow the vegetables to absorb the dressing, tossing gently from time to time to make sure all the vegetables are nicely coated.

Spoon the beets onto a platter and drizzle them with any dressing left in the bowl. Scatter the Gorgonzola and walnuts on top and serve.

Green Bean, Cherry Tomato, Corn, and Shallot Salad

Every year, I make this colorful salad in midsummer when all the star ingredients are in season at the farmers' market. If there is salad left over, I add pieces of ripe avocado and enjoy it for lunch the next day.

½ lb (225 g) green beans or a mix of green and wax beans, trimmed and cut into 1½-inch (4-cm) pieces (about 2 cups)

2 cups (340 g) cherry tomatoes (¾ lb), in a mix of colors, halved

2 cups (340 g) fresh corn kernels (from 3–4 ears), cooked, or frozen corn kernels, thawed

1 large shallot, halved lengthwise and sliced crosswise paper-thin

2 tablespoons white balsamic vinegar (see Cook's Note)

¼ cup (60 ml) extra-virgin olive oil

½ teaspoon fine sea salt

1 handful fresh basil leaves, torn

MAKES 4 SERVINGS

Fit a saucepan with a steamer basket and add water to the pan to reach just below the bottom of the basket. Bring to a boil over high heat, add the green beans, cover, and steam until the beans are tender and bright but not too soft, 5–6 minutes. Transfer the beans to a bowl.

Add the tomatoes, corn, and shallot to the bowl. Drizzle in the vinegar and oil and toss gently to coat evenly. Sprinkle with the salt and stir in the basil. Let the salad sit for 5–10 minutes so the flavors can mingle.

Spoon the salad into a decorative bowl and serve.

COOK'S NOTE
White balsamic vinegar is a variation of traditional balsamic vinegar. It's made from a blend of white grape must and white wine vinegar cooked down at a low temperature to prevent the color from darkening. It is sweet, fruity, and tart and is a great alternative to the darker variety when you don't want to muddy the colors of your salad.

PASTA

RICE

POLENTA

Cavatelli with Walnut Pesto

Cavatelli are bite-size ovals of pasta with a groove in the center that is perfect for capturing sauce. They are one of the easiest—and most fun—pastas to make by hand. They call for just two ingredients, fine semolina flour and water, and can be made without any special equipment. If pressed for time, you can substitute store-bought cavatelli. Walnut pesto is not the traditional sauce for this shape (tomato sauce is), but it's one of my favorites for the way the creamy ricotta and walnut sauce richly coats each shape.

DOUGH

2 cups plus 2 tablespoons (300 g) semola rimacinata (fine semolina flour), plus more for dusting

¾ cup (180 ml) water, at room temperature

WALNUT PESTO

¼ cup (30 g) walnut halves

1 small clove garlic

½ teaspoon fine sea salt, plus more for the pasta water

5 fresh basil leaves, chopped

Leaves from 1 small fresh marjoram sprig

1 tablespoon extra-virgin olive oil

Freshly ground white or black pepper

1 cup (225 g) whole-milk ricotta cheese, well-drained

Freshly grated Parmigiano Reggiano cheese, for serving

MAKES 4 SERVINGS

To make the dough, pour the flour into a mound on a clean work surface. A wooden pasta board is ideal but not necessary. Using your knuckles and the back of your hand, make a wide, shallow well in the center of the mound. Slowly pour the water into the well, taking care not to let it spill over the walls. Using a fork or your fingers, begin to incorporate the flour into the water, pulling the flour from the inside wall of the well. Continue to incorporate the flour until the mixture is first a slurry, then a thick batter, and finally a rough dough. At this point, switch to your hands and begin kneading the dough together. Use a dough scraper to scrape bits from the work surface and incorporate them into the dough. Continue to bring the dough together and knead it until you have incorporated most or all of the flour and the dough has a nice, firm, bouncy consistency (like a baby's bottom!). Knead a few minutes more until the dough is smooth and supple. Cover tightly and let rest at room temperature for at least 30 minutes or up to several hours.

Dust a large sheet pan with flour for the cavatelli once they are shaped. Slice off a golf ball–sized piece of dough and roll it out into a rope about the thickness of your pinkie. Cut the rope into nuggets ½–¾ inch (12 mm–2 cm) long. Grasp 1 nugget with your thumb and index and middle fingers and gently but firmly drag it toward you. This will create a two-fingered indentation in the piece of dough on one side and a roughish surface on the other. This is your first cavatello. Continue to shape the rest of the nuggets the same way and transfer them to the prepared sheet pan. Make sure the cavatelli are not touching or they will stick together. Continue cutting, rolling, and shaping until you have shaped all the dough. Cover the cavatelli with clean kitchen towels while you make the pesto (see the Cook's Note for longer storage).

To make the walnut pesto, preheat the oven to 350°F (180°C). Spread the walnuts on a small sheet pan or a pie pan and toast until they have taken on color and are fragrant, about 7 minutes. Transfer the walnuts to a mortar, preferably marble, and let cool. Add the garlic and salt to the walnuts and, using a pestle, pound to a coarse paste. Add the basil and marjoram leaves and drizzle in the oil. Gently pound and stir with the pestle until thoroughly combined. Add a few grindings of pepper and stir well. Add the ricotta to the mortar by the spoonful, stirring to incorporate it with the other ingredients. Once you have added all the ricotta, give the pesto a vigorous stir to make it light and fluffy. Taste and add more salt and pepper if needed. Transfer to a serving bowl large enough to incorporate the pasta. (A food processor or blender can be used in place of the mortar and pestle. First pulse the cooled walnuts to grind them, then add the garlic, salt, basil, marjoram, oil, and pepper and process or blend to mix well. Add the ricotta and process or blend briefly to incorporate. Transfer to the serving bowl and give the mixture a vigorous stir to make it light and fluffy.)

To cook the pasta, bring a large pot of water to a rolling boil and salt it generously. Carefully slide in the cavatelli, return the water to a boil, and cook, stirring once or twice, until al dente, 5–7 minutes. The pasta will float to the surface when it's almost done. Taste to make sure it is al dente and has no raw flour taste.

Use a spider or large slotted spoon to transfer the pasta to the serving bowl holding the pesto. Add a ladleful of the cooking water and stir to incorporate the pasta and water with the pesto, adding another ladleful of the water if needed for a good consistency. Stir in a couple of tablespoons of Parmigiano, adding another splash or two of cooking water if needed to loosen the sauce.

Transfer the pasta to individual bowls. Sprinkle each serving with a little Parmigiano and serve.

COOK'S NOTE
Both the cavatelli and the pesto can be made in advance. To store the cavatelli, arrange them on the semolina-dusted sheet pan as directed and freeze until solid, about 2 hours. Transfer the cavatelli to a lock-top plastic freezer bag or an airtight container and store in the freezer for up to 1 month. To cook, transfer the cavatelli straight from the freezer to the boiling water. Do not thaw them before cooking or they will stick together.

The pesto will keep in a tightly lidded container in the refrigerator for up to 3 days.

Spirals with Trapanese Pesto

Trapani, on the western coast of Sicily, is famous for its ancient salt works and its tuna fishing. More recently, it's become known for pesto alla trapanese, a ground almond and herb sauce that is Sicily's answer to Genoa's famous emerald-hued basil pesto. Like Genoese pesto and walnut pesto (see page 56), this is a "raw" sauce. The ingredients are mixed to a smooth paste in a food processor (or more traditionally, pounded in a mortar) and then tossed with hot cooked pasta, some grated pecorino, and a few splashes of starchy pasta water to help loosen things up.

12 cherry tomatoes

½ cup (70 g) raw almonds

1 cup (30 g) firmly packed fresh young basil leaves, plus a few leaves for garnish

¾ cup (20 g) lightly packed fresh mint leaves, plus a few leaves for garnish

1 handful arugula

2 small cloves garlic, coarsely chopped

Fine sea salt and freshly ground black pepper

About ½ cup (120 ml) extra-virgin olive oil

1 package (1 lb/450 g) gemelli, fusilli, or cavatappi pasta

Freshly grated pecorino romano cheese, for serving

MAKES 4 SERVINGS

Preheat the oven to 375°F (190°C). Bring a small saucepan filled with water to a boil over high heat. Cut an X on the blossom end of each tomato and plunge half of the tomatoes into the boiling water just long enough to loosen their skins, 30–60 seconds. Using a slotted spoon, transfer them to a bowl to cool slightly. Repeat with the remaining tomatoes. Leave the water boiling on the stove top.

Add the almonds to the boiling water and blanch until their skins loosen, 2–3 minutes. Drain and transfer them to a separate bowl to cool slightly.

Peel the skins off of the tomatoes, gently squeeze out any seeds, and set the tomatoes aside. Pop the almonds out of their skins and spread the nuts on a small sheet pan or a pie pan. Place in the oven to dry out and to toast lightly, about 7 minutes. Do not allow them to brown. Pour onto a plate and let cool.

Put the almonds, basil, mint, and arugula in a food processor. Scatter the garlic over the top and season with ½ teaspoon salt and a grinding of pepper. Add the tomatoes and pulse to break up the ingredients. With the motor running, drizzle in enough oil to achieve a thick, nearly (but not quite) smooth paste. Scrape the pesto into a bowl and season to taste with salt and pepper. Cover and set aside.

Bring a large pot of water to a rolling boil and salt it generously. Drop in the pasta, stir to separate, and cook until al dente, according to the package instructions.

Recipe continues

Spirals with Trapanese Pesto continued

Drain the pasta, reserving about 1 cup (240 ml) of the cooking water. Return the pasta to the pot and scrape in most of the pesto (reserve a few tablespoons) and a handful of pecorino. Pour in a splash of the reserved pasta water and toss vigorously to combine everything well. If the sauce is thick and clumpy, add more pasta water to loosen it up until it coats the pasta evenly.

Transfer the pasta to individual bowls. Top each bowl with a dollop of the reserved pesto and a sprinkle of pecorino and serve.

COOK'S NOTE

To make the pesto in a mortar, pound together the nuts, garlic, salt, and pepper to a paste. Pound in the herbs and tomatoes until fully incorporated. While stirring constantly, slowly drizzle in the oil and then continue to stir until a thick, not-quite-smooth, spoonable sauce forms. Make sure the oil is thoroughly mixed into the other ingredients. Season to taste with salt and pepper.

Spaghetti with Fresh Tomato Sauce

Every few weeks I get a craving for spaghetti al pomodoro, which is nothing more than pasta dressed with plain tomato sauce. This is a strictly summer sauce to make with meaty plum tomatoes that have ripened in the heat and sun. Use home-grown tomatoes or those from the farmers' market—supermarket tomatoes won't do here. The technique I use to prep the tomatoes—grating them on the large holes of a box grater—is slightly tedious, but it makes a fine pulp that's just right for sauce.

2 ½–3 lb (1.1–1.4 kg) meaty
plum tomatoes

¼ cup (60 ml) extra-virgin olive oil

1 clove garlic, lightly crushed

Fine sea salt

1 fresh basil sprig with numerous
leaves attached, plus 4–5 leaves

1 package (1 lb/450 g) spaghetti

Freshly grated Parmigiano
Reggiano cheese, for serving

MAKES 4 SERVINGS

Set a sieve over a bowl. Cut the tomatoes in half lengthwise and scoop out the seeds with your fingers, dropping them into the sieve. Press against the seeds with the back of a spoon to extract any liquid. Discard the seeds and set aside the liquid.

Stand a box grater on a cutting board with a moat to catch the juices as you grate. Holding the cut side of a tomato half flat against the large holes of the grater, grate the tomato, pressing gently, until only the skin is left, then discard the skin. As you work, transfer the pulp to a bowl, tipping in the juices as well.

In a large saucepan or deep frying pan over medium heat, cook the oil and garlic for about 2 minutes, pressing down on the garlic to release its flavor. Pour in the tomatoes and their juices—watch out for spattering oil—and stir to coat them with the oil. Season with ½ teaspoon salt, raise the heat to medium-high, and bring to a simmer. Lay the basil sprig on top, reduce the heat to medium-low, and simmer uncovered, stirring from time to time, until the oil pools on the surface and the sauce is nicely thickened but still fresh tasting, 25–30 minutes. Remove from the heat and discard the basil sprig, then tear the basil leaves into pieces and stir them into the sauce. Just before serving, reheat gently over medium-low heat.

Bring a large pot of water to a rolling boil and salt it generously. Drop in the spaghetti, stir to separate, and cook until al dente, according to the package instructions. Drain the pasta, reserving about 1 cup (240 ml) of the cooking water.

Return the spaghetti to the pot and spoon in about three-fourths of the hot sauce, tossing to coat the noodles evenly. Add a splash of reserved cooking water if ncessary to loosen the sauce.

Transfer the pasta to individual bowls, spoon the remaining sauce on top, and serve. Pass the cheese at the table.

Bucatini Cacio e Pepe

People love to weigh in on the "best" technique for making this classic Roman dish. I've always relied on elbow grease to stir the grated pecorino cheese into a creamy sauce that beautifully coats the fat noodles without clumping. Don't skimp on the pepper; you really need to go overboard.

2 tablespoons black peppercorns

Fine sea salt, for cooking the pasta

1 package (1 lb/450 g) bucatini

¼ lb (115 g) pecorino romano cheese, grated (preferably on a Microplane)

MAKES 4 SERVINGS

In a small frying pan over medium-high heat, toast the peppercorns, shaking the pan often, until fragrant, 2–3 minutes. Pour into a mortar and let cool to room temperature, then pound with a pestle until coarsely ground. (If you prefer, you can skip this step and use freshly ground black pepper, but be sure to grind it yourself. Ground pepper from a shaker or canister won't be nearly fragrant or potent enough.)

Bring a large pot of water to a rolling boil and salt it generously. Drop in the bucatini, stir to separate the noodles, and cook until slightly underdone—very al dente—according to the package instructions. It will finish cooking in the pot.

Drain the pasta, reserving about 1 cup (240 ml) of the cooking water. Don't let the pasta drain fully, however. While it is still dripping wet, return it to the pot and set over low heat. Pour in one-third of the reserved cooking water and stir with a pasta fork until the pasta has absorbed some of the liquid. Then stir more vigorously, adding in the cheese—reserve a little for serving—as you stir. Add a splash more cooking water and 1 tablespoon of the ground pepper and keep stirring until the strands are nicely coated with a creamy sauce, adding more cooking water if needed to loosen the sauce.

Transfer the pasta to individual bowls. Top with the reserved pecorino and a little more pepper and serve.

Guitar-Cut Spaghetti with Zucchini and Saffron Cream

An end-of-summer dish if ever there were one, with crispy pieces of pancetta and sliced zucchini slowly cooked down to a lovely sauce richly tinged with red-gold saffron and cream. Spaghetti alla chitarra is the traditional noodle from Abruzzo, my mom's home region. You need a special utensil, a wooden frame strung with parallel metal wires called a chitarra *(guitar), to make it, or the chitarra attachment for a pasta machine. However, this sauce works just as well with 1 pound (450 g) good-quality packaged pasta. Rustichella d'Abruzzo and La Molisana both market high-quality spaghetti alla chitarra. Either way, don't leave out the final touch: a shower of freshly grated Parmigiano Reggiano cheese.*

DOUGH

1 cup plus 2 scant tablespoons (150 g) semola rimacinata (fine semolina flour), plus more for dusting

1 cup plus 2 scant tablespoons (150 g) "00" pasta flour or unbleached all-purpose flour

3 extra-large eggs, at room temperature

SAUCE

Generous pinch of saffron threads (½–1 teaspoon)

1 tablespoon hot water

2 tablespoons extra-virgin olive oil

¼-lb (115-g) piece pancetta, diced

2 cloves garlic, lightly crushed

6 small-to-medium zucchini, quartered lengthwise, then cut crosswise into pieces ¼ inch (6 mm) thick

Fine sea salt and freshly ground black pepper

½ cup (120 ml) heavy cream

5 large fresh basil leaves

Freshly grated Parmigiano Reggiano cheese, for finishing and serving

MAKES 4 SERVINGS

To make the dough, in a food processor, combine the flours and pulse briefly to mix. Add the eggs and pulse until the mixture forms large curdlike crumbs. Turn the mixture out onto a clean work surface and gather it together to form a rough ball. Then knead for several minutes until the dough forms a smooth, stiff ball. Place a bowl over the dough or wrap it tightly in plastic wrap and let rest at room temperature for 1 hour.

Dust a work surface with semolina flour. Set up a hand-crank pasta machine or fit a stand mixer with the pasta roller attachment. Cut the dough into quarters and rewrap 3 quarters. Roll out the remaining quarter into a flat oval on the floured work surface. Starting with a narrow end, pass the oval through the roller on the widest setting. Fold the dough into thirds and, starting with an open, narrow end, pass it through the roller again. Repeat the folding and rolling through the widest setting two more times until the dough is a smooth, even rectangle. Now reset the roller to the next narrowest setting and pass the dough through the roller twice, then adjust the roller to the next narrowest setting. Continue to pass the dough through the roller twice on each setting until you have a long, thin sheet about ⅛ inch (3 mm) thick—thicker than is normal for, say, tagliatelle. Lay the sheet on the floured work surface and let it dry slightly while you roll out the remaining pieces of dough the same way.

Line a large sheet pan with a clean kitchen towel and dust with semolina flour. If using a traditional chitarra utensil, trim the sheets of pasta so they are 2 inches (5 cm) shorter than its length. (Save the trimmings in plastic wrap and reroll once to make one more sheet of pasta.) Place a sheet on the chitarra. With a small rolling pin, roll back and forth over the dough, pressing it first gently and then more firmly as you go, to cut the noodles. A wooden tray in the bottom of the chitarra catches the noodles as they fall through the wires. (You can "strum" the chitarra to help the noodles drop.) Tip out the noodles, sprinkle them liberally with semolina, wrap them around your hand to form a nest, and set the nest on the prepared sheet pan. Cut the remaining pasta sheets the same way and set them on the sheet pan.

If using a pasta machine with a chitarra attachment, pass the pasta sheets through the cutter, form the noodles into nests, and set on the prepared sheet pan.

Recipe continues

COOK'S NOTE
The noodles can be made ahead of time and frozen. Put the sheet pan with the nests in the freezer and freeze until the noodles are solid, at least 1 hour. Transfer the noodles to a lock-top plastic freezer bag or an airtight container and store in the freezer for up to 1 month. To cook, transfer the noodle nests straight from the freezer to the boiling water. Do not thaw before cooking or they will stick together.

Check the pasta. If the nests look like they might start sticking or clumping together, place the sheet pan in the freezer while you make the sauce. (See the Cook's Note for longer storage.)

To make the sauce, put the saffron threads into a mortar. (The amount you use depends on how forward you want the saffron flavor.) Using a pestle, pound the saffron to a powder. (Alternatively, use a heavy object, such as the smooth side of a meat mallet, to break up the threads.) Scrape the saffron into a small bowl and stir in the hot water. Let the mixture steep while you continue with the sauce.

In a large frying pan, warm the oil over medium heat. Drop in the pancetta and sauté, stirring from time to time, until the pancetta has rendered some of its fat and is slightly crispy, about 8 minutes. Reduce the heat to medium-low, stir in the garlic, and cook, stirring occasionally, until it starts to sizzle, about 2 minutes. Do not let it brown. Press down on the garlic to release its flavor, then remove and discard. Stir in the zucchini and season with a pinch of salt (the pancetta is salty, so go easy) and a generous amount of pepper. Cook slowly over medium-low heat, gently tossing from time to time, until the zucchini is completely tender and some of the pieces soften to a pulpy consistency, about 30 minutes. Stir in the saffron and its liquid and the cream and cook, stirring occasionally, until slightly thickened, about 3 minutes longer. Remove from the heat. Tear the basil leaves, dropping them into the sauce, and stir well. Just before the pasta is ready, reheat gently over medium-low heat.

Bring a large pot of water to a rolling boil and salt it generously. Drop the noodle nests into the boiling water and stir to separate them. Return the water to a boil and cook until al dente, 2–3 minutes. (If using packaged pasta, cook until al dente according to the package instructions.) Drain the pasta, reserving about 1 cup (240 ml) of the cooking water.

Transfer the pasta to the frying pan and gently toss with the sauce, adding a handful of Parmigiano and a splash or two of the reserved cooking water if needed to loosen the sauce.

Transfer the pasta to individual bowls and serve. Pass the cheese at the table.

Penne all'Arrabbiata

I admit to a slight bias toward this quill-shaped pasta, as it holds sauce so well (and, coincidentally, it shares the name of the town in Abruzzo where my family has a small house). We Abruzzesi love our hot pepper, so I make this extra spicy. A condiment called Bomba Calabrese is my secret weapon. It is a mixture of finely minced chile, eggplant, artichoke, and mushroom preserved in sunflower oil. You can find it at markets that sell Italian products and online.

¼ cup (60 ml) extra-virgin olive oil

1 clove garlic, lightly crushed

¼ teaspoon red pepper flakes

2 tablespoons Bomba Calabrese (optional)

1 can (28 oz/800 g) whole tomatoes with juices, crushed with your hands or a potato masher

Fine sea salt

1 tablespoon finely chopped fresh flat-leaf parsley

1 package (1 lb/450 g) penne

Freshly grated pecorino romano cheese, for finishing and serving

MAKES 4 SERVINGS

In a large frying pan over medium heat, cook the oil and garlic for about 2 minutes, pressing down on the garlic to release its flavor. Add the red pepper flakes and Bomba Calabrese, if using, and stir until the mixture begins to sizzle. Stir in the tomatoes and their juices (watch for spatters) and season to taste with salt. Raise the heat to medium-high and bring to a simmer. Lower the heat to medium-low and cook at a gentle simmer until nicely thickened, 20–25 minutes. Remove from the heat and stir in the parsley. Just before the pasta is ready, reheat gently over medium-low heat.

Bring a large pot of water to a rolling boil and salt it generously. Drop in the penne, stir to separate, and cook until al dente according to the package instructions. Drain the pasta, reserving about 1 cup (240 ml) of the cooking water.

Transfer the pasta to the frying pan and gently toss with the sauce, adding a small handful of pecorino and a splash or two of the reserved cooking water if needed to loosen the sauce.

Transfer the pasta to individual bowls and serve. Pass the cheese at the table.

Bow Ties with Summer Cherry Tomato Sauce and Mozzarella

The beauty of this sauce is in its simplicity. Just four main ingredients—cherry tomatoes, olive oil, garlic, and basil—and a minimal amount of time in a pan produce a robust sauce that clings beautifully to pasta.

Coarse sea salt, for cooking the pasta

¼ cup (60 ml) extra-virgin olive oil

1–2 cloves garlic, sliced paper-thin

1 small fresh red chile (peperoncino), thinly sliced crosswise, or pinch of red pepper flakes

4 cups (680 g) cherry tomatoes (1½ lb)

1 teaspoon fine sea salt

1 handful fresh basil leaves or mix of fresh basil and mint leaves, torn

1 package (1 lb/450 g) bow tie pasta

1 ball (8 oz/225 g) milky fresh mozzarella cheese, torn into small pieces

Freshly grated Parmigiano Reggiano cheese, for serving

MAKES 4 SERVINGS

Bring a large pot of water to a rolling boil and salt it generously with coarse salt.

While the water is heating, in a large frying pan over medium-low heat, combine the oil, garlic, and chile (if using) and cook, stirring occasionally, until the garlic is softened but not browned, about 5 minutes. Gently drop in the tomatoes and toss to coat them with the oil. Season with the fine sea salt, raise the heat to medium-high, and bring to a simmer. Cook, uncovered, until the tomatoes have burst and collapsed and the sauce has thickened, about 15 minutes. Reduce the heat to medium or medium-low if necessary to keep the sauce at a gentle simmer. Taste and adjust the seasoning with fine salt if needed. Remove from the heat, stir in the basil, and cover to keep warm.

Drop the bow ties into the boiling water, stir to separate, and cook until al dente, according to the package instructions. Drain the pasta, reserving about 1 cup (240 ml) of the cooking water.

Transfer the pasta to the frying pan and gently toss with the sauce, adding a splash or two of the reserved cooking water if needed to loosen the sauce. Sprinkle in the mozzarella and toss again until the cheese softens slightly and starts to become stringy.

Transfer the pasta to individual bowls and serve. Pass the Parmigiano at the table.

Tagliatelle with Short Rib Ragù

Fresh tagliatelle sauced with rich beef ragù is an affordable luxury. This dish takes a while to prepare, but it's a good project for a winter weekend, and it will perfume your house with the scent of rosemary and bay. If you don't have time to make the noodles, you can substitute 1 pound (450 g) dried tagliatelle.

DOUGH

2 cups (250 g) "00" pasta flour or unbleached all-purpose flour, or equal parts of each, plus more if needed and for dusting

1 tablespoon semolina flour, "00" pasta flour, or unbleached all-purpose flour, plus more for dusting

3 extra-large eggs, at room temperature

RAGÙ

2 tablespoons sunflower or other neutral oil

2 lb (1 kg) meaty beef short ribs

Fine sea salt and freshly ground black pepper

1–2 tablespoons extra-virgin olive oil, if needed

2 medium carrots, peeled and finely chopped (about 1 cup/140 g)

2 celery ribs, finely chopped (about 1 cup/140 g)

1 red onion, finely chopped (about 1 cup/140 g)

1 tablespoon finely chopped fresh rosemary

1 fresh bay leaf

To make the dough, in a food processor, combine the flours and pulse briefly to mix. Add the eggs and pulse until the mixture forms curdlike crumbs. Pinch together a bit of the mixture; it should form a soft ball. If it seems dry, dribble in a little water by the teaspoon and pulse until the dough starts to come together. If it is too soft and sticky, add more "00" flour, 1 tablespoon at a time, and pulse until the dough starts to come together. This is important: It is fine if the dough is a little tacky, as you will be kneading more flour into it. It is easier to add flour to sticky dough than to add liquid to dry dough.

Turn the dough out onto a work surface (preferably wood as, unlike pie dough, pasta dough loves a warm surface) lightly dusted with "00" flour. Knead the dough using the palm and heel of your hand, pushing the dough gently but firmly away and then folding it over toward you. Rotate the dough a quarter turn and repeat the pushing and folding motion. Continue to knead, rotating the dough a quarter turn each time, until it is smooth and silky, about 6 minutes. Form the dough into a ball and place a bowl over it or wrap it tightly in plastic wrap. Let rest at room temperature for 30–60 minutes.

Dust a work surface with "00" flour. Set up a hand-crank pasta machine or fit a stand mixer with the pasta roller attachment. Cut the dough into quarters and re-cover or rewrap 3 quarters. Roll out the remaining quarter into a flat oval on the floured work surface. Starting with a narrow end, pass the oval through the roller on the widest setting. Fold the dough into thirds and, starting with an open, narrow end, pass it through the roller again. Repeat the folding and rolling through the widest setting two more times until the dough is a smooth, even rectangle.

1 cup (240 ml) Dolcetto d'Alba or other dry, fruity red wine

1 cup (240 ml) water

1 cup (240 g) tomato passata (purée)

Freshly grated Parmigiano Reggiano cheese, for serving

MAKES 4–6 SERVINGS

Reset the roller to the next narrowest setting and pass the dough through the roller twice, then adjust the roller to the next narrowest setting. Continue to pass the dough through the roller twice on each setting until you have a long, thin sheet between 1/16 and 1/8 inch (2 and 3 mm) thick. You should just be able to see the shadow of your hand through it. Lay the sheet on the floured work surface to dry slightly while rolling out the remaining pieces of dough.

Line a sheet pan with a kitchen towel and dust with semolina flour. To cut the tagliatelle, sprinkle a sheet of dough with semolina flour and roll it up, jelly roll–style. Cut the roll crosswise into ribbons 1/4 inch (6 mm) wide. Fluff the ribbons with your fingers to unravel them and set them in a mound on the prepared sheet pan. Repeat with the remaining pasta sheets. (Alternatively, you can use a tagliatelle cutter attachment on your pasta machine or stand mixer.)

Let the tagliatelle air-dry while you make the ragù. Be sure to fluff them now and again to make sure they are not sticking together. Or to prevent sticking, you can place the sheet pan in the freezer while you make the ragù.

To make the ragù in a large Dutch oven over medium heat, warm the sunflower oil. Season the short ribs lightly with salt and pepper and arrange them in the pot without crowding them (you may need to work in batches). Cook the ribs, turning once, until nicely browned on both sides, about 4 minutes on each side. Transfer the ribs to a platter. If there is a lot of fat in the pot, discard all but 2 tablespoons. If there is very little, add 1–2 tablespoons olive oil.

Reduce the heat to medium-low and stir in the carrots, celery, and onion. Add the rosemary and bay leaf and cook, stirring until the vegetables are softened and golden, 8–10 minutes. Raise the heat to medium-high and pour in the wine. Let it bubble for a minute or two, then stir in the water and tomato passata. Season with 1 teaspoon salt and a few grindings of pepper. Return the ribs to the pot along with any juices on the platter. Bring to a boil, reduce the heat to medium-low, and cover. Braise the ribs, turning them every now and then and reducing the heat if necessary to maintain the gentlest of simmers, until the meat is fall-off-the-bone tender, 2–2 1/2 hours.

Recipe continues

***Tagliatelle with Short Rib Ragù** continued*

Remove from the heat and transfer the ribs to a cutting board. Let cool until they can be handled, then strip the meat from the bones, chop it coarsely, and return it to the sauce. Cover and reheat over low heat.

Bring a large pot of water to a rolling boil and salt it generously. Drop the noodles into the boiling water and stir to separate them. Return the water to a boil and cook until al dente, 2–5 minutes. (If using packaged pasta, cook until al dente according to the package instructions.) Drain the pasta, reserving about 1 cup (240 ml) of the cooking water.

Return the pasta to the pot and spoon in some of the ragù. Toss gently, coating the noodles well and adding a splash or two of the reserved cooking water if needed to loosen the sauce.

Transfer the pasta to individual bowls and spoon more ragù on top. Sprinkle with Parmigiano and serve.

COOK'S NOTE
Another way to serve this rich dish is to remove the ribs from the sauce, dress the tagliatelle with the meat-infused sauce, and then serve the ribs as a second course. Or save the meat from the ribs (it can be frozen) and use it as a filling for ravioli.

Mezze Maniche with Ricotta, Pancetta, and Black Pepper

I've come to think of this as a "cheater's" version of carbonara, with fresh ricotta standing in for the eggs. Make sure the pepper is freshly ground and use lots of it—enough to make your nose itch as you're grinding.

6-oz (170-g) piece pancetta, cut into small cubes

¾ cup (170 g) fresh whole-milk ricotta cheese

¼ cup (60 g) smoked whole-milk ricotta cheese or additional fresh ricotta cheese

Finely grated zest of 1 lemon

Fine sea salt and freshly ground black pepper

1 package (1 lb/450 g) mezze maniche (half sleeves) pasta or other short, sturdy shape, such as rigatoni or penne

4 tablespoons (30 g) freshly grated Parmigiano Reggiano or pecorino romano cheese, for serving

MAKES 4 SERVINGS

Line a plate with paper towels. Put the pancetta into a cold large frying pan and set over medium heat. Cook, stirring from time to time, until the pancetta has rendered some of its fat and is browned and slightly crispy but still tender, about 8 minutes. Using a slotted spoon, transfer the pancetta to the towel-lined plate to drain. Remove the pan from the heat and discard all but 2 tablespoons of the fat from the pan.

In a bowl, combine the fresh ricotta, smoked ricotta (if using), and lemon zest and stir vigorously to mix well and soften the ricotta.

Bring a large pot of water to a boil and salt it generously. Drop the mezze maniche into the boiling water, stir to separate, and cook until slightly underdone—very al dente—according to the package instructions. (It will finish cooking in the frying pan.) Drain the pasta, reserving about 1 cup (240 ml) of the cooking water.

Transfer the pasta to the frying pan and toss it with the fat in the pan. Add a splash of the reserved cooking water and set the pan over medium-low heat to finish cooking the pasta. Stir in the ricotta mixture and more cooking water as needed to make a creamy sauce that coats the mezze maniche. Season generously with pepper and with more salt if needed.

Transfer the pasta to individual bowls. Top each bowl with 1 tablespoon of the Parmigiano and more pepper and serve.

Fettuccine with Truffled Cheese

Let's face it: not all of us have fresh truffles stashed in our pantry, waiting to be shaved over pasta. Sottocenere al tartufo, a semisoft cow's milk cheese flecked with black truffle, makes a nice substitute, infusing a creamy sauce with that heady aroma. If you can't find it, use fontina Valle d'Aosta and add a drop or two of truffle oil. Fettuccine are the same width as tagliatelle but slightly thicker. Either noodle works well in this recipe.

2 tablespoons unsalted butter

⅓ cup (50 g) finely diced sweet onion, such as Maui, Vidalia, or Walla Walla (about ¼ onion)

1 cup (240 ml) heavy cream

½ teaspoon fine sea salt, plus more for cooking the pasta

Freshly ground black pepper

2 tablespoons mascarpone

1 cup (115 g) shredded sottocenere al tartufo cheese

1 package (1 lb/450 g) fettuccine, or 1 batch homemade tagliatelle (see page 70)

½ cup (60 g) freshly grated Parmigiano Reggiano cheese, plus more for serving

MAKES 4 SERVINGS

In a large frying pan over medium-low heat, melt the butter. Add the onion and cook, stirring often, until the onion is soft and translucent, 8–10 minutes.

Pour in the cream and season with the salt and a few grindings of pepper. Raise the heat to medium and simmer until the cream has reduced and thickened slightly, about 10 minutes. Gently whisk in the mascarpone until melted. Turn off the heat and stir in the sottocenere al tartufo until melted. Taste and adjust the seasoning with salt if needed. Cover to keep warm.

Bring a large pot of water to a rolling boil and salt it generously. Drop in the pasta, stir to separate, and cook until al dente. If using the fettuccine, cook according to the package instructions. If using the homemade tagliatelle, the pasta will be ready in 2–5 minutes.

Using tongs, transfer the pasta to the pan of warm sauce. Turn the heat on low and gently toss the noodles with the sauce until well coated. Sprinkle in half of the Parmigiano and a little more pepper and toss again.

Transfer the pasta to individual bowls and serve. Pass additional Parmigiano at the table.

Winter Polenta with Taleggio

In Italy's smallest region, Valle d'Aosta, which is tucked into the northwest corner of the country, polenta is more than a pantry staple. It is a daily ritual, the same way a dish of pasta fills that role for many people in southern Italy. In Aosta itself, a cozy alpine city ringed with mountains, polenta is featured on every ristorante and osteria menu, whether topped with grilled sausage or carbonada valdostana (beef stew) or with lots of melty cheese stirred in. Use a blend of fine- and medium-grind polenta, as they do in Aosta. Serve the polenta as is or topped with sausage, beef stew, or braised greens. This is a rich dish, so it can stretch further than four servings.

1 cup (150 g) medium-grind stone-ground polenta

½ cup (75 g) fine-grind stone-ground polenta

6–7 cups (1.4–1.7 l) water, plus more if needed

2 teaspoons fine sea salt

½ lb (225 g) Taleggio cheese, including the rind, cut into small pieces

4 tablespoons (115 g) unsalted butter

MAKES 4 OR MORE SERVINGS

Pour the polenta into a heavy-bottomed saucepan and whisk in 6 cups (1.4 l) water and the salt. Set over medium-high heat and bring to a boil, stirring often. Reduce the heat to maintain a gentle bubbling and cook, continuing to stir often to prevent the polenta from sticking or scorching on the bottom of the pan, for 45–50 minutes. The polenta is ready when it is thick and creamy but still pourable. If you find it is too thick toward the end of cooking, stir in a little more water.

Remove the pot from the heat, add the Taleggio, and stir until completely melted and incorporated. Stir in the butter until melted, then spoon into shallow bowls and serve.

Lemon-Ricotta Ravioli with Lemon Cream Sauce

Sorrento and the towns along the Amalfi Coast are famous for their beaches, profusion of flowers, staggering cliffs, and narrow coastal roads with hairpin turns. The food is fresh and zesty—tomatoes, garlic, seafood, and lemons. Sorrento's aromatic and sweet lemons are known the world over, and they appear in many dishes, both sweet and savory. This sauce is typically served with spaghetti or spaghettini but also makes the perfect pairing for ravioli.

DOUGH

2 cups (250 g) plus 2 tablespoons "00" pasta flour or unbleached all-purpose flour, plus more if needed

3 extra-large eggs, at room temperature

Semolina flour, "00" pasta flour, or unbleached all-purpose flour, for dusting

FILLING

2 cups (1 lb/450 g) whole-milk ricotta cheese, well drained (see Cook's Note, page 79)

½ cup (60 g) freshly grated Parmigiano Reggiano cheese

Finely grated zest of 1 small lemon

½ teaspoon fine sea salt

Pinch of freshly ground black pepper

the flour into a food processor, add the eggs, and pulse until the mixture forms small curdlike crumbs. Pinch together a bit of the mixture; it should form a soft ball. If the mixture seems dry, dribble in a little water by the teaspoon and pulse until the dough starts to come together. If the mixture is too soft and sticky, add more flour, 1 tablespoon at a time, and pulse until the dough starts to come together.

Turn the dough out onto a lightly floured work surface, preferably wood (unlike pie dough, pasta dough loves a warm surface). Knead the dough using the palm and heel of your hand, pushing the dough gently but firmly away and then folding it over toward you. Rotate the dough a quarter turn and repeat the pushing and folding motion. Continue to knead, rotating the dough a quarter turn each time, until it is smooth and silky, about 6 minutes. Form the dough into a ball and place a bowl over it or wrap it tightly in plastic wrap. Let rest at room temperature for 30–60 minutes.

While the dough rests, make the filling. In a bowl, combine the ricotta, Parmigiano, lemon zest, salt, and pepper. Fold together, mixing well, then cover and refrigerate until ready to use.

Dust a work surface with semolina flour. Set up a hand-crank pasta machine or fit a stand mixer with the pasta roller attachment. Cut the dough into quarters and re-cover or rewrap 3 quarters. Roll out the remaining quarter into a flat oval on the floured work surface. Starting with a narrow end, pass the oval through the roller on the widest setting. Fold the dough into thirds and, starting with an open, narrow end, pass it through the roller again. Repeat the folding and rolling through the widest setting two more times until the dough is a smooth, even rectangle.

Recipe continues

¼ cup (60 ml) extra-virgin olive oil

Finely grated zest of 1 lemon

1 cup (240 ml) heavy cream

¼ teaspoon fine sea salt

2 tablespoons fresh lemon juice

Freshly ground black pepper

Fine sea salt, for cooking
the pasta

FOR SERVING

1 tablespoon minced fresh
flat-leaf parsley

1 tablespoon minced fresh basil

Freshly grated Parmigiano
Reggiano cheese

MAKES 4 SERVINGS

To make the dough, put

Lemon-Ricotta Ravioli continued

Now reset the roller to the next narrowest setting and pass the dough through the roller twice, then adjust the roller to the next narrowest setting. Continue to pass the dough through the roller twice on each setting until you have a long, thin sheet between ⅟₁₆ and ⅛ inch (2 and 3 mm) thick. You should just be able to see the shadow of your hand through it. Lay the sheet on the floured work surface and cover it with a kitchen towel to prevent it from drying out while you roll out the remaining pieces of dough the same way. The sheets must remain moist and supple so you can shape and seal them.

Line 2 large sheet pans with clean kitchen towels and dust with semolina flour. Lay a sheet of dough on the work surface. Using a piping bag fitted with a small plain tip or a spoon, pipe or spoon 1-tablespoon mounds of the filling at 1-inch (2.5-cm) intervals along the length of the sheet, positioning the mounds along the center of the sheet half closest to you. Dip your finger in water and lightly moisten the edges of the dough sheet and the area between the mounds. Carefully fold the top half of the sheet over the filling, lining it up with the bottom edge of the sheet nearest you. Use your fingers to press out any air and seal the dough between the mounds and then press the edges of the dough firmly to seal. With a fluted pastry cutter, cut around the filling in a half-moon or rectangular shape. Or use a ravioli cutter or a cookie cutter to stamp out the shapes. Use the tines of a fork to seal the edges of the ravioli further (this is optional, but I like the pattern it creates). Transfer the ravioli to a prepared sheet pan, making sure they are not touching. Continue to fill and shape ravioli until you have used all of the dough. You should have about 48 ravioli.

If cooking the ravioli within a couple of hours, leave them be. Otherwise, put the sheet pans in the freezer until the ravioli are frozen solid, about 2 hours, then transfer them to lock-top plastic freezer bags or an airtight container and freeze for up to 1 month.

To make the sauce, pour the oil into a heavy-bottomed saucepan or frying pan and add the lemon zest. Set over low heat and cook, stirring every now and again, until the zest begins to sizzle. Stir in the cream and salt, raise the heat to medium-high, and bring to a simmer. Cook, stirring, until the cream thickens slightly, about 3 minutes. Slowly whisk in the lemon juice, 1 tablespoon at a time; the cream will thicken further. Season to taste with pepper, remove from the heat, and cover to keep warm.

While the sauce is cooking, bring a large, wide saucepan or shallow pot of water to a boil and salt it generously. Gently lower the ravioli into the water and cook until al dente, 3–5 minutes. (If necessary, cook them in batches to avoid crowding the pan.) Using a wire skimmer, transfer the cooked ravioli to a warmed platter or individual bowls.

Spoon the sauce over the ravioli, then sprinkle with the parsley, basil, and a dusting of Parmigiano and serve.

COOK'S NOTE

It is important that the ricotta be well drained. You will need to begin draining it before you start making the pasta dough. Line a large fine-mesh sieve with cheesecloth and set it over a bowl. Spoon the ricotta into the sieve, twist the ends of the cheesecloth together to enclose it, and set a weight on top. Let it drain for an hour or longer. (If draining only half the amount, drain for 30 minutes or so. By draining the ricotta, you lose about 25 percent of the original volume, so 1 cup (225 g) ricotta will yield about 3/4 cup (170 g) well-drained ricotta.

Fresh Corn and Zucchini Risotto

While not traditional, corn really takes well to risotto, especially when the kernels are freshly cut from the cob. The corn's starchy "milk" and sugars make already creamy risotto even creamier. After cutting the kernels from the cobs, be sure to run the back of the knife down the length of the cob to remove the milky bits clinging to the crevices. If corn is not in season, frozen kernels can be substituted.

4 tablespoons (60 g) unsalted butter

2 tablespoons extra-virgin olive oil

3 spring onions, white and pale green parts, thinly sliced; or 1 small white onion, finely diced

4 small-to-medium zucchini, quartered lengthwise, then thinly sliced crosswise

1 cup (170 g) fresh corn kernels, plus "milk" scraped from cobs (from 2 ears)

Finely grated zest of 1 lemon

Several fresh lemon or regular thyme sprigs

1½ cups (300 g) risotto rice, such as Arborio or Carnaroli

1 teaspoon fine sea salt

¼ cup (60 ml) dry white wine

6 cups (1.4 l) vegetable broth, chicken broth, or water, heated to a simmer

⅓ cup (80 ml) heavy cream

½ cup (50 g) fontina Valle d'Aosta

Freshly grated Parmigiano Reggiano cheese, for finishing and serving

MAKES 4–6 SERVINGS

In a large, heavy-bottomed saucepan over medium heat, heat the butter and oil. When the butter has melted and the mixture is sizzling, stir in the onions and cook, stirring often, until slightly softened, about 5 minutes. Stir in the zucchini and cook, stirring occasionally, until they start to soften, about 10 minutes. Add the corn and lemon zest, then gently rub the thyme sprigs between your fingers (to release their flavor) and add them to the pan. Stir in the rice and salt and toast, stirring often, until the grains are translucent, about 2 minutes.

Raise the heat to medium-high, pour in the wine, and stir until absorbed. Add about a ladleful of the hot broth—just enough to cover the rice—reduce the heat to medium, and stir until the broth is nearly absorbed. Stir in another ladleful of broth and continue to cook, stirring, until nearly absorbed. Continue adding the broth, a ladleful at a time and stirring until absorbed before adding more, until the rice is tender but still pleasantly chewy, 20–25 minutes. You should be able to see the transformation, especially toward the end of cooking. The rice will gradually plump up, turn white, and take on a creamy texture. When it is almost ready—it should be firm and a little chalky at the center (taste a few grains)—stir in the cream and then add the fontina and a handful of Parmigiano and continue to stir until the cheeses are fully incorporated. Stir in a final ladleful of broth to achieve a creamy texture. The risotto should be all'onda (wavy) and neither too stiff nor too runny, and it should mound softly on a spoon. Remove and discard the thyme sprigs.

Spoon the risotto into shallow bowls, top each bowl with a little more Parmigiano, and serve.

Venetian Rice and Peas with Baby Artichokes

Risi e bisi—*rice and peas—is traditionally served in Venice on April 25, both in honor of the feast day of Saint Mark and also to herald the arrival of spring and, with it, the first peas of the season. Unlike risotto, this dish, a thick soup, or* minestra, *doesn't require constant stirring, just a simmering of rice in a pea-scented chicken broth. It's gentle in flavor and just right for cool spring evenings. I've bucked tradition a bit by adding baby artichokes to the mix.*

2 lb (1 kg) English peas in the pod, or 2 cups (280 g) frozen peas

3 cups (700 ml) chicken broth, preferably homemade (page 38)

3¼ cups (740 ml) water

½ lemon

6 baby artichokes

3 tablespoons extra-virgin olive oil

1 small clove garlic, lightly crushed

3 teaspoons finely chopped fresh flat-leaf parsley

Fine sea salt

2 tablespoons unsalted butter

3 spring onions, white part only, or 1 small white onion, finely chopped

1½ cups (300 g) risotto rice, such as Vialone Nano or Carnaroli

1 fresh marjoram sprig

1 cup (115 g) freshly grated grana padano or Parmigiano Reggiano cheese (see Cook's Note)

Freshly ground black papper

MAKES 4 SERVINGS

Shell the peas and set aside in a bowl. You should have about 2 cups (280 g). Rinse the pods and put them into a saucepan along with the broth and 3 cups (680 ml) of the water. Bring to a boil over medium-high heat, then reduce the heat to medium-low or low, cover partially, and simmer gently until the broth is nicely infused with fresh pea flavor, 20–30 minutes. Strain the broth through a fine-mesh sieve and return it to the saucepan. Cover to keep warm.

In a small saucepan over medium heat, combine the peas and the remaining ¼ cup (60 ml) water and bring to a simmer. Cover and cook until bright green and just tender, about 6 minutes. Set aside off the heat.

If using frozen peas, put them into a bowl and let them thaw. In a saucepan over medium-high heat, combine the broth and the 3¼ cups (740 ml) water and bring to a boil. Remove from the heat and cover to keep warm.

To trim the artichokes, fill a bowl with water and squeeze in the juice from the lemon half. Working with 1 artichoke at a time, trim off the end of the stem, then peel off the tough outer layer of the stem. Pull off the tough outer leaves until you reach the smooth, tender lemon-colored leaves. Trim around the base of the leaves to remove any tough bits, then cut off the top half of the leaves. Cut the artichoke lengthwise into quarters and scoop out and discard any fuzzy choke. Immerse the artichoke quarters in the lemon water and repeat with the remaining artichokes, adding them to the lemon water.

Recipe continues

In a frying pan over medium heat, warm 2 tablespoons of the oil and the garlic clove and cook for about 2 minutes, pressing down on the garlic to release its flavor. Remove and discard the garlic. Drain the artichokes and add them to the pan, stirring to coat them with the oil. Sprinkle in 1 teaspoon of the parsley, ½ teaspoon salt, and a splash of the heated broth, then cover and cook at a simmer for 5 minutes. Uncover and continue to cook, stirring occasionally, until the artichokes are almost tender, about 5 minutes longer. Remove from the heat and set aside.

In a large Dutch oven or deep sauté pan over medium heat, warm the butter and the remaining 1 tablespoon oil until the butter is melted. Reduce the heat to medium-low and stir in the onions and the remaining 2 teaspoons parsley and cook, stirring often, until the onion is soft and translucent, 7–8 minutes. Stir in the rice, coating it well with the butter and oil and letting it toast until the grains are shiny, about 3 minutes. Add the marjoram, pour in the reserved hot broth, and raise the heat to medium-high. Bring to a boil, then reduce the heat to medium-low and cook at a gentle simmer, stirring to keep the rice from sticking to the bottom of the pot, for 10 minutes.

Add the peas and artichokes and cook until the vegetables are tender and the soup is thickened (there should still be some starchy liquid in the pot; add a splash of water if it's too dense), 5–10 minutes. Stir in half of the cheese and season with a grinding of pepper and another pinch of salt if needed.

Ladle the soup into shallow bowls. Top with the remaining cheese, dividing it evenly, and serve.

Piedmontese-Style Risotto with Prosecco

This is risotto at its essence—just a few ingredients, meaning they need to be top quality. Make sure to use "fresh" rice well within its expiration date (the oils in rice can turn it rancid quickly). Homemade broth is a must for this elegant dish. I don't often have fresh truffles at my disposal, but when one comes my way, this is how I like to showcase it.

4 tablespoons (60 g) unsalted butter

½ yellow onion, finely chopped (about ½ cup/70 g)

1½ cups (300 g) risotto rice, such as Carnaroli or Arborio

1 teaspoon fine sea salt

⅓ cup (80 ml) Prosecco

6 cups (1.4 l) homemade chicken broth (page 38), heated to a simmer

¼ cup (60 ml) heavy cream

Freshly grated Parmigiano Reggiano cheese, for finishing and serving

1 small black truffle, for serving (optional)

MAKES 4 SERVINGS

In a large, heavy-bottomed sauté pan over medium-low heat, melt the butter. When the butter is sizzling, stir in the onion and cook, stirring often, until softened but not browned, 7–8 minutes. Stir in the rice and salt and toast, stirring often, until the grains are translucent, about 2 minutes.

Raise the heat to medium-high, pour in the Prosecco, and stir until absorbed. Add about a ladleful of the hot broth—just enough to cover the rice—reduce the heat to medium, and stir until the broth is nearly absorbed. Stir in another ladleful of broth and continue to cook, stirring, until nearly absorbed. Continue adding the broth, a ladleful at a time and stirring until absorbed before adding more, until the rice is tender but still pleasantly chewy, 20–25 minutes. You should be able to see the transformation, especially toward the end of cooking. The rice will gradually plump up, turn white, and take on a creamy texture. When it is almost ready—it should be firm and a little chalky at the center (taste a few grains)—stir in a final ladleful of broth and the cream, followed by a handful of Parmigiano. The risotto should be all'onda (wavy) and neither too stiff nor too runny, and it should mound softly on a spoon.

Spoon the risotto into shallow bowls and top each bowl with a little more Parmigiano. If you have a truffle, shave a few slices onto each bowl and then serve.

Creamy Polenta with Summer Vegetable Stew

Polenta tends to be associated with cold-weather cooking. Served with ragù in Abruzzo, or with loads of melting fontina cheese stirred in, as is typical in Valle d'Aosta, a bowl of hot cornmeal porridge in winter is welcome comfort food. But polenta has a summer side too. This simple one-dish supper of custard-like polenta and jewel-toned stewed summer vegetables— tomatoes, green beans, peppers, and corn—showcases that side.

1 cup (150 g) fine-grind stone-ground polenta

2 ½ cups (600 ml) water

2 ½ cups (600 ml) whole or low-fat milk

Fine sea salt

Kernels from 2 ears corn (about 1 cup/170 g)

½ cup (60 g) packed freshly grated Parmigiano Reggiano cheese, plus more for serving

6 oz (170 g) small green beans, trimmed

¼ cup (60 ml) extra-virgin olive oil

1 red onion, cut into small dice

2 yellow bell peppers, seeded and cut into ½-inch (12-mm) pieces

2 cups (340 g) cherry tomatoes (¾ lb)

Freshly ground black pepper

1 handful fresh basil leaves, torn

MAKES 4 SERVINGS

Pour the polenta into a heavy-bottomed saucepan and whisk in the water, milk, and 1 teaspoon salt. Set over medium-high heat and bring to a boil, stirring often. Reduce the heat to maintain a gentle bubbling and cook, continuing to stir often to prevent the polenta from sticking or scorching on the bottom of the pan, for 45–50 minutes. The polenta is ready when it is soft and creamy but still pourable and not overly dense. About 10 minutes before it is done, stir in half of the corn kernels. At the end stir in Parmigiano, taste, and adjust the seasoning with salt if needed.

While the polenta is cooking, make the vegetable stew. Fit a saucepan with a steamer basket and add water to the pan to reach just below the bottom of the basket. Bring to a boil over high heat, add the green beans, cover, and steam until tender-crisp, 3–4 minutes. Remove from the heat, transfer the beans to a plate, and reserve.

In a large frying pan or sauté pan over low heat, combine the oil and onion and cook, stirring occasionally, until the onion is softened, about 7 minutes. Stir in the bell peppers, season with ½ teaspoon salt, and cook, stirring occasionally, until the peppers are tender, about 10 minutes. Tip in the cherry tomatoes and raise the heat to medium. Cook, stirring every now and then, until the tomatoes have started to burst and release their juices, about 5 minutes. Reduce the heat if necessary to prevent the vegetables from burning. Add the remaining corn kernels and the reserved green beans and cook until warmed through, about 5 minutes longer. Taste and season with ground pepper and with salt if needed.

Spoon the polenta into shallow bowls and top each serving with an equal amount of the stew. Top each bowl with a couple of tablespoons of Parmigiano and the basil and serve.

Baked Rigatoni with Eggplant

Do you know people who profess not to like eggplant? I do, but they all somehow love this baked dish of rigatoni tossed with simple tomato sauce and layered with stretchy smoked mozzarella. The salting and draining step is optional if you're using fresh, in-season eggplant, but I like the slightly compressed texture of the vegetable once it's gone through the process.

2 medium eggplants, about 1 lb (450 g) total weight

Kosher or fine sea salt

Extra-virgin olive oil

½ red onion, diced (⅓ cup/60 g)

1 clove garlic, lightly crushed

Generous pinch of red pepper flakes

1 can (28 oz/800 g) whole tomatoes with juices, crushed with your hands or a potato masher

1 handful fresh basil leaves, torn

1 package (1 lb/450 g) rigatoni

1 ball (½ lb/225 g) smoked mozzarella cheese, thinly sliced

½ cup (60 g) freshly grated Parmigiano Reggiano cheese

MAKES 6 SERVINGS

Trim the eggplants and cut them into ¾-inch (2-cm) cubes. Put the cubes into a colander set over a shallow bowl and sprinkle with salt, tossing to distribute the salt. Set a plate over the eggplants and weight it down with a heavy object (I use my marble mortar). Let drain for 30 minutes, then pat dry with a kitchen towel.

Line a large plate with paper towels. In a large frying pan over medium heat, warm ¼ cup (60 ml) oil. When the oil is hot, tip in half of the eggplant cubes and fry, turning them a couple of times, until golden brown, about 10 minutes. Using a slotted spoon, transfer the eggplant cubes to the towel-lined plate to drain. Repeat with the remaining eggplant cubes, adding more oil to the pan if needed.

In a heavy-bottomed saucepan over medium-low heat, warm ¼ cup (60 ml) oil and stir in the onion, garlic, and red pepper flakes. Cook, stirring often to prevent browning, until the onion is softened, about 7 minutes. Stir in the tomatoes (watch for spatters) and season with 1 teaspoon salt. Raise the heat to medium-high and bring to a boil, then reduce the heat and cook at a gentle simmer, stirring occasionally, until the sauce is somewhat thickened, about 20 minutes. Remove from the heat and stir in the basil and the fried eggplant cubes.

Preheat the oven to 400°F (200°C). Lightly coat a 9 x 13-inch (23 x 33-cm) baking dish with oil.

Bring a large pot of water to a rolling boil and salt it generously. Drop the rigatoni into the boiling water, stir to separate, and cook until slightly underdone—very al dente—according to the package instructions. (It will finish cooking in the oven.) Drain the pasta, reserving about ½ cup (120 ml) of the cooking water.

Transfer the pasta to the saucepan and gently toss with the sauce, mixing thoroughly and adding a splash of the pasta water if needed to loosen the sauce. Spoon half of the dressed pasta into the prepared baking dish. Arrange the mozzarella slices evenly over the top, then sprinkle evenly with half of the Parmigiano. Spoon the remaining dressed pasta over the cheese layer and sprinkle the remaining Parmigiano evenly on the top.

Bake, uncovered, until the cheese melts and is bubbly and the top is nicely browned and crisped in places, about 30 minutes. Let stand for 5 minutes before serving in shallow bowls.

COOK'S NOTE
If you'd like to get a head start on this recipe, the day before you plan to serve it, fry the eggplant and make the sauce and store them separately in tightly lidded containers in the refrigerator. Remove them from the refrigerator before you cook the pasta to bring them to room temperature, then proceed as directed with the recipe.

PIZZA

—————

FOCACCIA

Slow-Rise Pizza Dough

Giving pizza dough time to rise yields a much more flavorful crust. Most of the time here is hands-off. Just mix the dough in your food processor and set it aside to rest for a day or two. Your patience will be rewarded with excellent homestyle pizza with a crisp, light crust. (See the Cook's Note for a quick-rise version.)

1½ teaspoons fine sea salt

1¼ cups (300 ml) water

2 cups (250 g) unbleached all-purpose flour

¾ cup (95 g) bread flour

¼ cup (35 g) semolina flour

¼ teaspoon instant yeast (not rapid-rise)

Extra-virgin olive oil, for the bowl, your hands, and the sheet pan

MAKES ENOUGH DOUGH FOR ONE 11 X 17-INCH (28 X 43-CM) PIZZA; 4–6 SERVINGS

COOK'S NOTE
For a quick-rise pizza dough, increase the amount of yeast to 1 teaspoon. Let the dough rise at room temperature until doubled in size, about 2 hours.

In a small bowl, dissolve the salt in the water.

In a food processor, combine all the flours and the yeast and pulse briefly to mix. Add the salt water and pulse to mix, then process until all the ingredients come together to form a sticky dough, about 30 seconds. (The dough can also be mixed in a stand mixer fitted with the dough hook on medium-low speed.)

Lightly oil a bowl or a container with a lid, then lightly oil your hands. Pull the dough out of the processor and gather it together, turning and folding it a couple of times with oiled hands to form a ball. Place the dough in the prepared bowl or container and cover with plastic wrap or with the lid. Set it aside at room temperature to rise for at least 12 hours or preferably 24 hours to develop the flavor. (If not using after the rise, place the dough in the refrigerator for up to 2 days. Remove it several hours before using to bring it to room temperature.)

To shape the dough, use your hands to coat the bottom and sides of an 11 x 17-inch (28 x 43-cm) sheet pan with 2 tablespoons oil. Remove the pizza dough from its container and drop it gently onto the center of the pan. Lift the dough gently from underneath and pull it out toward the edges of the pan. (It may snap back, which is fine.) Cover with plastic wrap or clean reusable wrap and let it rest for 10 minutes. Then stretch it out again until it covers most of the pan. For a rectangular pizza, stretch the dough all the way to the edges; for an oval pizza, leave the corners of the dough rounded. Cover again and let it rest and puff up while the oven or grill heats and you prepare the remaining ingredients.

Use the dough as directed in individual recipes.

Pizza Margherita

Sporting the colors of the Italian flag, this pizza is one of Italy's most iconic and beloved contributions to world cuisine. This version is my home cook's adaptation, meant to be baked in a home oven. You can use a pizza stone or baking steel to drive up the heat intensity, but even without it, you'll still end up with a delicious, classic tomato pie.

Slow-Rise Pizza Dough (page 92)

1 cup (240 g) tomato passata (purée)

3 tablespoons extra-virgin olive oil

1 small clove garlic, lightly crushed

10 to 12 fresh basil leaves

½ teaspoon fine sea salt

2 balls (½ lb/225 g each) fresh (but not too milky) mozzarella cheese, thinly sliced

MAKES ONE 11 X 17-INCH (28 X 43-CM) PIZZA; 4–6 SERVINGS

Make, proof, and shape the dough as directed.

Position an oven rack in the top third of the oven and slide in a pizza stone or baking steel, if using. Preheat the oven to 500°F (260°C) for at least 45 minutes.

Put the tomato passata into a bowl, drizzle in the oil, and drop in the garlic. Tear 4 of the basil leaves into pieces and drop them into the bowl. Add the salt, stir to mix well, and set aside to allow the flavors to blend while the oven preheats.

Scoop out and discard the garlic from the tomato mixture, then spread the tomato mixture over the dough, leaving a 1-inch (2.5-cm) border uncovered. Slide the pizza into the oven using a pizza peel and bake until the dough is puffed but still pale and the tomato topping has thickened up a bit, about 6 minutes.

Remove the pizza from the oven and quickly arrange the mozzarella slices on top. Slide it back into the oven and bake until the crust is browned along the edges and the cheese is melted and browned in spots, about 5 minutes.

Remove from the oven and let cool briefly, then slice into rectangles or wedges and serve.

Roasted Pepper and Soppressata Pizza

Soppressata is a specific type of salami produced in several regions of Italy, most notably in Calabria. It is distinct for its coarse grind and for its somewhat flattened, oblong shape, which it gets from being weighted down during the curing process. Although it can be either sweet or spicy, I almost always opt for the latter, especially when pairing it with peppers on pizza.

Slow-Rise Pizza Dough (page 92)

1 cup (240 g) tomato passata (purée)

2 tablespoons extra-virgin olive oil

1 clove garlic, lightly crushed

4 fresh basil leaves

½ teaspoon fine sea salt

2 red bell peppers

2 balls (½ lb/225 g each) fresh (but not too milky) mozzarella cheese, thinly sliced

6 oz (170 g) thinly sliced hot (spicy) soppressata

MAKES ONE 11 X 17-INCH
(28 X 43-CM); 4–6 SERVINGS

Make, proof, and shape the dough as directed.

Put the tomato passata into a bowl and drizzle in 1 tablespoon of the oil. Drop in the garlic and the basil, season with the salt, and stir to combine.

Position an oven rack in the top third of the oven and preheat the broiler. Line a small sheet pan with aluminum foil, set the peppers on it, and slip the pan under the broiler. Broil the peppers, turning them with tongs every few minutes, until they are partially blackened and blistered on all sides, about 10 minutes total. Transfer the peppers to a bowl and cover with a kitchen towel. Let steam for 10 minutes.

Using an oven mitt, move the oven rack to the lower-middle of the oven, switch the setting to bake, and slide in a pizza stone or baking steel, if using. Preheat the oven to 500°F (260°C) for at least 45 minutes.

Gently pull off the stems from the peppers and pour out any liquid. Cut the peppers in half lengthwise and scrape away the seeds and membranes. Lay the halves, skin side up, on a cutting board and scrape away the charred skins with a paring knife. Cut each half lengthwise into narrow strips. Scoop the strips into a bowl and drizzle with the remaining 1 tablespoon oil.

Scoop out and discard the garlic from the tomato mixture, then spread the tomato mixture over the dough, leaving a 1-inch (2.5-cm) border uncovered. Lay the mozzarella slices on top of the sauce, followed by the soppressata and peppers.

Reduce the oven temperature to 450°F (230°C) and slide the pizza into the oven. Bake until the cheese is melted and browned in spots and the soppressata is sizzling, 20–25 minutes.

Remove from the oven and let cool briefly, then slice into rectangles or wedges and serve.

Pancetta and Caramelized Onion Pizza

Properly caramelizing onions takes time, but it is time well spent, as nothing quite matches their satiny texture and rich, sweet-savory flavor. They are the perfect counterpoint to the salty cubes of pancetta in this "white" (tomato-free) pizza.

Slow-Rise Pizza Dough (page 92)

2 tablespoons unsalted butter

4 tablespoons (60 ml) extra-virgin olive oil

2 lb (1 kg) sweet onions, such as Maui, Vidalia, or Walla Walla, halved and very thinly sliced

1 teaspoon fine sea salt

2 teaspoons finely minced fresh marjoram, oregano, flat-leaf parsley, or thyme or a mix

2 teaspoons dry Marsala

¼-lb (115-g) piece pancetta, thickly sliced, then cut into ⅓–½-inch (9–12-mm) dice

1 ball (½ lb/225 g) fresh (but not too milky) mozzarella cheese, cut into ½-inch (12-mm) dice

MAKES ONE 11 X 17-INCH
(28 X 43-CM); 4–6 SERVINGS

Make, proof, and shape the dough as directed.

Position an oven rack in the lower-middle of the oven and slide in a pizza stone or baking steel, if using. Preheat the oven to 500°F (260°C) for at least 45 minutes.

In a large Dutch oven or heavy-bottomed sauté pan over medium heat, warm the butter and 2 tablespoons of the oil. When the butter has melted, add the onions and stir to coat with the butter and oil. Reduce the heat to medium-low, sprinkle in the salt, and stir well. Cover and cook for 10 minutes to wilt the onions. Uncover and stir in the herbs, then reduce the heat to low, cover partially, and cook, stirring often, until the onions are reduced, silken in texture, and golden brown. This will take at least 45 minutes and probably closer to 1–1½ hours. When the onions are ready, stir in the Marsala and cook for a few minutes longer to incorporate the wine. Taste and adjust the seasoning. Remove from the heat and scrape the onions into a bowl.

While the onions are cooking, cook the pancetta. Scatter the pancetta pieces in a dry frying pan and set over medium heat. Cook, turning often, until the pancetta has rendered some of its fat and is slightly crisped, 7–10 minutes. Remove from the heat and scrape the pancetta into a small bowl.

Brush the remaining 2 tablespoons oil on the dough and scatter the mozzarella pieces evenly on top, leaving a 1-inch (2.5-cm) border uncovered. Spread the onions over the cheese and top evenly with the pancetta.

Reduce the oven temperature to 450°F (230°C) and slide the pizza into the oven. Bake until the crust is browned around the edges, the cheese is melted, and the pancetta is crispy, 20–25 minutes.

Remove from the oven and let cool briefly, then slice into rectangles or wedges and serve.

Grilled Fresh Herbs and Fontina Pizza

In summer, I like to turn my grill into a makeshift pizza oven. Thin rounds of dough cook quickly on the hot grates, and the pizzas turn out beautifully charred and crispy.

Slow-Rise Pizza Dough (page 92)

Extra-virgin olive oil, for coating the dough

Semola rimacinata (fine semolina flour) or all-purpose flour, for dusting

4 oz (115 g) fresh (not milky) mozzarella, thinly sliced

4 oz (115 g) shredded Fontina Val d'Aosta cheese (about 2 cups)

Freshly ground black pepper

2 medium ripe summer tomatoes, sliced into thin rounds

1 small red onion, halved and cut into paper-thin slices

1 cup (150 g) purple olives (Kalamata, Gaeta, or Taggiasca), pitted and halved

1 cup (about 1 ounce/28 g) baby arugula

1 cup (1 oz/28 g) mixed fresh herbs, such as basil and mint

Olio nuovo (page 181), for drizzling

Flaky sea salt, for serving

MAKES TWO 12-INCH PIZZAS;
4–6 SERVINGS

Make and proof the dough as directed on page 92, but do not shape it. After its slow rise, remove the dough from refrigerator and cut it into 2 equal pieces. From each piece into a ball, coat them lightly with olive oil, and set them in separate bowls or containers. Cover with plastic or reusable wrap and let come to room temperature.

Prepare a fire in a charcoal grill or preheat a gas grill to high. If using charcoal, spread the hot coals across one half of the bottom of the grill and leave the other half clear to create a cool zone. If using gas, turn one of the burners to low. Lightly oil the grill grate.

On a lightly floured work surface, stretch a piece of dough into a thin circle about 12 inches (30 cm) in diameter. Carefully transfer the round to a baking sheet lightly dusted with flour and cover with a piece of parchment paper. Stretch the second piece of dough and transfer it to the parchment paper. Cover with a second piece of parchment.

Have your toppings ready and near the grill. Brush one side of a dough round with olive oil and place it, oiled side down, on the hot part of the grill. Grill just until grill marks form on the bottom and the crust begins to puff up and turn crispy, about 2 minutes. Using tongs and a wide spatula, flip the pizza and move it to the cool area of the grill. Top with half the mozzarella and fontina, and half the tomato slices. Scatter half the olives and onions on top, cover, and grill until the bottom of the pizza is browned and crisp and the cheese has melted, 3 to 5 minutes. Transfer to a cutting board. Make the second pizza in the same way.

Top each grilled pizza with the arugula and herbs. Drizzle with a thread of olio nuovo and sprinkle with flaky salt. Cut into wedges and serve.

Rapini and Scamorza Pizza

Welcome to the pizza of my dreams. It features two of my favorite foods in the universe: smoked scamorza, a "drier" version of mozzarella from Abruzzo that melts beautifully, and pungent rapini cooked with lots of garlic. If you can't find scamorza, use smoked mozzarella.

Slow-Rise Pizza Dough (page 92)

5 tablespoons (75 ml) extra-virgin olive oil

2 cloves garlic, sliced paper-thin

2 bunches rapini (broccoli rabe), about 1 lb (450 g) total weight, tough stems discarded and rinsed but not dried

Generous pinch of red pepper flakes

1 teaspoon fine sea salt

1 ball (½ lb/225 g) smoked scamorza or smoked mozzarella cheese, thinly sliced

1 ball (½ lb/225 g) fresh (but not too milky) mozzarella cheese, thinly sliced

MAKES ONE 11 X 17-INCH
(28 X 43-CM) PIZZA;
4–6 SERVINGS

Make, proof, and shape the dough as directed.

Position an oven rack in the lower-middle part of the oven and slide in a pizza stone or baking steel, if using. Preheat the oven to 500°F (260°C) for at least 45 minutes.

In a large frying pan over medium-low heat, combine 3 tablespoons of the oil and the garlic and cook, stirring occasionally, until the garlic is softened but not browned, 5–7 minutes. Add the rapini by the handful, with the water still clinging to its leaves. If it doesn't all fit into the pan, cover the pan and let it wilt briefly before adding more. Sprinkle in the red pepper flakes and salt, cover, and cook, stirring from time to time, until the rapini is tender, about 20 minutes. Uncover and continue to cook until the greens are very tender and most of the liquid has evaporated, about 10 minutes.

Drizzle the remaining 2 tablespoons oil on the dough and strew the rapini on top, leaving a 1-inch (2.5-cm) border uncovered. Arrange the scamorza and mozzarella slices on top.

Reduce the oven temperature to 450°F (230°C) and slide the pizza into the oven. Bake until the crust is browned around the edges and the cheese is melted and browned in spots, 20–25 minutes.

Remove from the oven and let cool briefly, then slice into rectangles or wedges and serve.

Mortadella, Stracciatella, and Pistachio Pizza

Silky mortadella is the star of this unconventional and elegant pizza enriched with a green topping of pistachio pesto and dappled with stracciatella, a creamy cheese made of mozzarella shreds mixed with cream. Bonus: If you have any leftover pesto, you can extend it with more basil and another clove of garlic and turn it into a sauce for pasta.

Slow-Rise Pizza Dough (page 92)

PISTACHIO PESTO

Generous 1½ cups (200 g) raw pistachios

1 clove garlic, coarsely chopped

1 teaspoon fine sea salt

1 small handful fresh young basil leaves (about ½ cup/15 g)

⅓–½ cup (80–120 ml) extra-virgin olive oil

½ cup (60 g) freshly grated Parmigiano Reggiano cheese

2 tablespoons extra-virgin olive oil

1 ball (½ lb/225 g) fresh (but not too milky) mozzarella cheese, cut into small cubes

8 large, thin slices mortadella

½ lb (225 g) stracciatella cheese, or 1 ball (½ lb/225 g) burrata cheese, skin and filling chopped together

MAKES ONE 11 X 17-INCH (28 X 43-CM) PIZZA; 4–6 SERVINGS

Make, proof, and shape the dough as directed.

Position an oven rack in the lower-middle part of the oven and slide in a pizza stone or baking steel, if using. Preheat the oven to 500°F (260°C) for at least 45 minutes.

To make the pesto, in a food processor, combine the pistachios, garlic, salt, and basil and pulse until the nuts are coarsely chopped. With the motor running, drizzle in just enough oil to make a thick, spoonable sauce. Scrape the pesto into a small bowl and stir in the Parmigiano. Cover and set aside.

Drizzle the 2 tablespoons oil over the dough and scatter the mozzarella cubes evenly on top, leaving a 1-inch (2.5-cm) border uncovered. Slide the pizza into the oven and bake until the crust is puffed and beginning to brown and the mozzarella is melted and is browned in spots, about 18 minutes.

Remove the pizza from the oven and spread the pesto over the surface, again leaving a 1-inch (2.5-cm) border uncovered. Arrange the mortadella slices on the pesto, not flat but rather like casually strewn handkerchiefs with folds and some height. Return the pizza to the oven just until the pesto and mortadella are warm, 1–2 minutes.

Remove from the oven and top with dollops of the stracciatella. Let cool briefly, then slice into rectangles or wedges and serve.

Barese-Style Potato Focaccia, page 106.

Pancetta and Caramelized Onion Pizza, page 97

Pizza Carbonara

The same ingredients in Rome's iconic spaghetti alla carbonara—*eggs, guanciale, and lots of black pepper—make a spectacular pizza. Serve this rich concoction with a simple salad of bitter greens. Any leftover white sauce is delicious tossed with pasta.*

Slow-Rise Pizza Dough (page 92)

WHITE SAUCE

3 tablespoons butter

1 large shallot, finely chopped (about ¼ cup/35 g)

¼ cup (60 ml) dry white wine

1 cup (240 ml) heavy cream

¼ cup (30 g) freshly grated pecorino romano cheese

¼ teaspoon fine sea salt

Freshly ground black pepper

¼-lb (115-g) piece guanciale or pancetta, cut into ½-inch (12-mm)

1 ball (½ lb/225 g) fresh (but not too milky) mozzarella cheese, thinly sliced

¼ cup (30 g) freshly grated pecorino romano cheese

Freshly ground black pepper

Fine sea salt

6 large eggs, at room temperature

MAKES ONE 11 X 17-INCH (28 X 43-CM) PIZZA; 4–6 SERVINGS

Make, proof, and shape the dough as directed.

Position an oven rack in the lower-middle part of the oven and slide in a pizza stone or baking steel, if using. Preheat the oven to 500°F (260°C) for at least 45 minutes.

To make the white sauce, in a heavy-bottomed saucepan over medium heat, melt the butter. Stir in the shallot and cook, stirring often, until slightly softened, about 5 minutes. Raise the heat to medium-high, pour in the wine, and let it bubble until almost evaporated. Pour in the cream and bring to a boil. Reduce the heat to a gentle simmer and cook, stirring, until thickened, 15–20 minutes. Stir in the cheese and season with the salt and a generous grinding of pepper. Cook, stirring often, until the cheese is melted, 2–3 minutes. Remove from the heat and cover.

Line a small plate with a paper towel. Put the guanciale into a cold frying pan (preferably cast iron) and set over medium heat. Cook, stirring occasionally, until the pieces are somewhat browned and just beginning to crisp, about 6 minutes. Using a slotted spoon, transfer to the towel-lined plate.

Spread the white sauce over the dough, leaving a 1-inch (2.5-cm) border uncovered. Arrange the mozzarella slices over the sauce and scatter the guanciale pieces evenly over the top. Sprinkle with the pecorino and season generously with pepper.

Slide the pizza into the oven using a pizza peel and bake until the cheese is melted and the top of the pizza and edges of the crust are beginning to brown and bubble, about 10 minutes.

Remove from the oven and turn the oven to broil. Using an oven mitt, slide the oven rack to the top third of the oven. Crack the eggs onto the pizza, spacing them well to keep them separate. Sprinkle the yolks with pinches of salt and pepper. Return the pizza to the oven and broil until the eggs are just set but the yolks are still runny, 3–4 minutes.

Remove from the oven and let cool briefly, then slice into rectangles or wedges and serve.

Potato and Rosemary Pizza

My mom's three sisters shared an apartment in Rome's northeast quadrant, near Villa Ada. Not far from their apartment was a classic Roman rosticceria, *where we occasionally bought a rotisserie chicken and fried potatoes for lunch. The place also sold* pizza al taglio, *which is pizza baked in large rectangular pans and sold in square or rectangular slices. My favorite was the pizza of thin, overlapping slices of potato perfumed with rosemary, tender in some spots and crunchy in others. Heaven.*

Slow-Rise Pizza Dough (page 92)

1 tablespoon fine sea salt

2 medium yellow or red potatoes, about 10 oz/280 g total weight

1 rounded tablespoon fresh rosemary leaves

3 tablespoons extra-virgin olive oil

Freshly ground black pepper

1 ball (½ lb/225 g) fresh mozzarella cheese, cut into small cubes

MAKES ONE 11 X 17-INCH (28 X 43-CM) PIZZA; 4–6 SERVINGS

Make, proof, and shape the dough as directed.

Position an oven rack in lower-middle part of the oven and slide in a pizza stone or baking steel, if using. Preheat the oven to 500°F (260°C) for at least 45 minutes.

Fill a bowl with tepid water and dissolve the salt in the water. Slice the potatoes as thinly as possible. (I use a mandoline, but a sharp chef's knife works.) Immerse the potato slices in the salt water and let them soak until they lose their crispness, 30–60 minutes. Drain them into a colander set in the sink, then spread them in a single layer on a kitchen towel. Cover with another kitchen towel and pat dry.

In a small bowl, toss the rosemary with the oil.

Arrange the potato slices in rows on top of the dough, overlapping them slightly and leaving a ½-inch (12-mm) border uncovered. Spoon the rosemary leaves and oil onto the potatoes, spreading the mixture evenly. Season with a liberal grinding of pepper and scatter the mozzarella cubes on top.

Reduce the oven temperature to 450°F (230°C) and slide the pizza into the oven. Bake until the crust is browned along the edges, the cheese is melted, and the cheese and potatoes are browned in spots, 20–25 minutes.

Remove from the oven and let cool briefly, then slice into rectangles or wedges and serve.

Barese-Style Potato Focaccia

This round focaccia from Bari, in Puglia, the heel of Italy's boot, is unique. It contains lots of semolina flour, which gives it a golden hue, and a mashed potato, which enriches the dough. A good bit of olive oil is also used, in the dough and to oil the pans. Don't skimp here, as it's the oil that gives the focaccia its signature crunchy edges and bottom.

1 small-to-medium yellow potato, about 5 oz(140 g)

Fine sea salt

1½ cups (350 ml) water

2 cups (250 g) unbleached all-purpose flour, as needed and more for dusting

1½ cups (210 g) semola rimacinata (fine semolina flour)

½ teaspoon instant yeast (not rapid-rise)

1 tablespoon extra-virgin olive oil, plus more for the bowls, pans, and brushing

12 large cherry tomatoes, halved

24 cured olives or purple brined olive, such as Gaeta

1–2 teaspoons crushed dried oregano

Flaky sea salt

MAKES TWO 9-INCH (23-CM) ROUND FOCACCE; 4–6 SERVINGS

In a small saucepan, combine the potato with water to cover and salt the water with fine salt. Bring to a boil over medium-high heat and cook the potato until tender, about 20 minutes. Drain and let cool until it can be handled, then pass it through a ricer or peel it and mash well with a fork or potato masher. You should have ½ cup (130 g). Let cool.

Dissolve 2 teaspoons fine salt in the water and reserve.

In the bowl of a stand mixer, combine both flours and the yeast and use a spatula or whisk to mix well. Fit the mixer with the dough hook. Add the mashed potato to the bowl, then pour in the salt water, followed by the oil. Mix on low speed to bring the ingredients together, then increase the speed to medium-high and mix until a soft dough forms. If the dough is very sticky, add more all-purpose flour, 1 tablespoon at a time. Don't add too much flour, as this is meant to be a soft dough.

Turn the dough out onto a lightly floured work surface and cut it in half. Flour your hands lightly and form each half into a ball. Coat 2 bowls with oil. Place a dough ball in each bowl and turn the balls to coat them with oil. Cover the bowls with a kitchen towel and let the dough rise at room temperature until doubled in size, 3–4 hours. Refrigerate the dough overnight.

The next day, generously coat the bottom and sides of two 9-inch (23-cm) round cake pans with oil. Remove the dough from the refrigerator and put a portion, still cold, into each prepared pan, spreading it evenly. Cover with a kitchen towel and let rise in a warm spot until doubled in height and nicely puffed, about 4 hours.

Preheat the oven to 450°F (230°C). Brush the top of the dough in each pan with oil. Gently press half of the cherry tomato halves, cut side up, and half of the olives into the dough in each pan, distributing them evenly. Sprinkle with the oregano and with flaky salt.

Bake the focacce until golden brown and crispy on top, 20–25 minutes. Turn out onto wire racks and then turn right side up. Enjoy warm or at room temperature, cut into squares.

Ligurian Focaccia

It's not an overstatement to say that Ligurian focaccia (also known as focaccia alla genovese *and* fügassa all'euio*) is revered throughout the region and beyond. It is part of the Slow Food Presidia, a project devoted to safeguarding local food traditions in Italy and around the world. Crispy around the edges and soft in the center, a thin, salt-encrusted slice of focaccia (plain or onion topped) dipped into cappuccino is the way many Ligurians begin their day.*

SPONGE

¼ teaspoon instant yeast (not rapid-rise) or active dry yeast

¼ cup (60 ml) water, at room temperature

¾ cup (95 g) bread flour

DOUGH

2 ½–2 ¾ cups (315–345 g) unbleached all-purpose flour, plus more as needed and for dusting

2 teaspoons instant yeast (not rapid-rise)

2 teaspoons sugar

1½ teaspoons fine sea salt

Sponge (see above)

¾ cup (180 ml) cold water

7–8 tablespoons (105–120 ml) extra-virgin olive oil

BRINE

¾ cup (180 ml) water

1½ teaspoons fine sea salt

MAKES 1 LARGE FOCACCIA; 10–12 SERVINGS

Start the sponge the night before you plan to make the focaccia. In a bowl, stir together the yeast and room-temperature water. Add the bread flour and knead to form a ragged dough. Transfer the dough to a bowl or jar small enough so the dough touches the sides and can grow vertically. Cover with plastic wrap and let sit at room temperature until doubled in height, 12–14 hours.

To make the dough, combine 2 ½ cups (315 g) of the all-purpose flour, the yeast, sugar, and salt in the bowl of a stand mixer. Add the sponge and cold water and stir briefly with a wooden spoon. Fit the mixer with the dough hook and mix on low speed until a shaggy dough starts to form, about 2 minutes. Add 2 tablespoons of the oil and continue to mix on low until the oil is absorbed. Increase the speed to medium-low and knead until the dough is more or less smooth, about 5 minutes. If it feels sticky, sprinkle in a little more flour.

Transfer the dough to a clean work surface and knead by hand, adding a little more flour only if it's still sticky, until smooth and elastic, about 5 minutes. (If you like, you can do the entire kneading process by hand rather than in the mixer, but the dough is somewhat stiff, so you'll need a lot of elbow grease.)

Form the dough into an oblong about 8 x 10 inches (20 x 25 cm) long and then fold it into thirds, as you would a business letter. Give the dough a quarter turn, stretch it into an oblong again, and again fold it into thirds. Pat and press it into a rounded rectangle and set it aside on a lightly floured surface. Cover with a kitchen towel or plastic wrap and let rest for 45 minutes.

Pour 1 tablespoon of the oil into the center of an 11 x 17-inch (28 x 43-cm) sheet pan. With a pastry brush, oil the bottom of the pan, taking care to leave a 2-inch (5-cm) border around the perimeter uncovered and adding a little more oil if needed to cover. Lightly flour the dough and roll it out into a rectangle about ½ inch (12 mm) thick. Transfer it to the prepared sheet pan. It won't cover the entire surface. Cover the dough with a clean kitchen towel or plastic wrap and let rise for 30 minutes.

Now, with your fingers, lift the dough from underneath and gently pull it, stretching it until it reaches the edges of the pan. If it's not stretching easily, re-cover it and let it rest for 10 minutes before stretching it again. Press the dough into the edges of the pan, making sure there are no gaps. (This step will keep the brine from seeping underneath the focaccia during baking.) Re-cover the dough and let rise in a warm spot until puffed, about 1 hour.

To make the brine, pour the water into a small microwave-safe bowl and heat in a microwave on 50 percent power until warm (about 105°F/40°C), 30–60 seconds. Add the salt and stir until completely dissolved. Place the sheet pan in front of you, with a short side facing you. Dust the dough lightly with flour. With the first, second, and third fingers of both hands, and starting at the top left, press down firmly into the dough, pressing with the pads of your fingers to create elongated dimples. Working in rows, continue down the length of the dough until the entire surface is dimpled. Carefully pour the brine over the dough, taking care to distribute it as evenly as possible. It will seem like too much liquid, but it will be absorbed during baking. Drizzle 2 tablespoons of the oil evenly over the surface. Let the dough rise, uncovered, for 45 minutes. About 20 minutes before the dough has completed this final rise, preheat the oven to 450°F (230°C).

Bake the focaccia until the edges and parts of the surface are golden brown but the dimples are still tending toward pale beige, about 20 minutes. Remove from the oven and brush the surface with the remaining 2 tablespoons oil. Use a long offset spatula to dislodge the focaccia from the pan. As soon as the oil and any lingering brine are absorbed, turn the focaccia upside down onto a wire rack to prevent the bottom from getting soggy. Let cool briefly before cutting into rectangles. Enjoy warm.

COOK'S NOTE
My thanks go to Ligurian chef and sommelier Valentina Venuti, who taught a tour group I led how to make this iconic flatbread, and to Laurel Evans, author of *Liguria: The Cookbook* and a longtime resident of the region, whose recipe was also a guideline. Please don't be intimidated by the lengthy instructions. It's not difficult to make, and once you've done it a couple of times and gotten the feel of the dough, it's fairly easy. If you can, use Ligurian olive oil, which has a mild, buttery flavor.

Whole-Wheat Focaccia with Sweet Onion and Sage

This is a slow-rise focaccia, one that I like to prepare on a chilly fall weekend. The whole process takes two to three days, but it's well worth the wait, as the slow rise allows the flavor of the dough to develop. Onion and sage make a wonderful fall topping for this whole-wheat focaccia. Using a sweet onion, such as Maui, Vidalia, or Walla Walla, balances the rich, savory flavor of the sage leaves.

DOUGH

2 ½ cups (315 g) whole-wheat flour

2 ½ cups (315 g) unbleached all-purpose flour

2 teaspoons fine sea salt

½ teaspoon instant yeast (not rapid-rise)

1 ¾ cups plus 2 tablespoons (455 ml) warm water (105°–110°F/41°–43°C)

3 tablespoons extra-virgin olive oil, plus more as needed for your hands and the pan

2 teaspoons runny honey

TOPPING

2 cups (200 g) thinly sliced sweet onions

3 tablespoons extra-virgin olive oil

¼ teaspoon fine sea salt

1 tablespoon thinly sliced fresh sage leaves (chiffonade), plus 8–12 whole leaves

1 ½ teaspoons coarse sea salt

Freshly coarse-ground black pepper

MAKES 1 LARGE FOCACCIA; 8 OR MORE SERVINGS

To make the dough, in the bowl of a stand mixer, combine both flours, the salt, and the yeast and use a spatula or whisk to mix well. Fit the mixer with the paddle attachment. With the mixer on low speed, slowly pour in two-thirds of the water and mix until absorbed. Drizzle in the oil and honey, pour in the remaining water, increase the speed by one notch, and continue to mix the dough until all the liquid is absorbed. The dough will wrap itself around the paddle, which is fine. Turn off the mixer and use a sturdy spatula to scrape the dough off the paddle. The dough will be somewhat sticky.

Lightly coat a work surface and your hands with about 1 tablespoon oil. Lift the dough out of the bowl and set it on the oiled surface. Knead the dough briefly to smooth it out, pushing it away from you and then folding it over toward you and giving it a quarter turn. Repeat this sequence until the dough is smooth. Then flip the dough over so the seam is on the bottom and rotate it with your hands to create a smooth ball. Focaccia dough is somewhat slack, so the ball of dough won't be very tight; this is fine. Lightly oil a bowl or plastic container and transfer the dough to it, turning the dough to coat it with oil. Cover with plastic wrap or a lid and let the dough rise in a warm spot until at least tripled in size. (I use a 6-qt/5.7-l Cambro plastic tub with a lid.) The amount of time it takes the dough to rise will depend on how warm the ambient temperature is. I usually leave the dough on top of the stove, under the hood light, for 3–4 hours.

Transfer the covered bowl or container to the refrigerator and let the dough rest for 24–36 hours. When you are ready to bake, remove it from the refrigerator and let it sit for 3 hours to come to room temperature.

Use your hands to coat the bottom and sides of an 11 x 17-inch (28 x 43-cm) sheet pan with 2 tablespoons oil. With oiled hands, gently coax the dough out of the bowl or container, using your fingers to pry it away from the sides, and let it fall softly onto the center of the prepared pan. Without pressing, fold the dough lightly into thirds, like a business letter, to achieve a rough rectangular shape, patting it gently to even it out. Cover with plastic wrap and let sit for 30 minute.

Carefully work your hands under the dough and stretch it gently toward the edges of the pan. Try to stretch it evenly so it is the same thickness all over. If the dough resists, let it relax for a few minutes longer. Do this stretching and relaxing a few times over the course of 15–30 minutes, until the dough fills the pan to the edges and corners. Cover the dough with plastic wrap and let rise until it puffs up, 30–45 minutes.

While the dough is rising on the sheet pan, prepare the topping. In a bowl, combine the onions, 1 tablespoon of the oil, the fine salt, and sliced sage leaves and mix well to coat everything with the oil. Let marinate until the onions release their liquid and soften, about 30 minutes.

Uncover the dough and poke it all over with your fingers to create dimples. Spread the onion and sage mixture evenly over the dough and drizzle the onion liquid from the bowl on top. Cover again and let sit for another 30–60 minutes to puff up once more. While the dough is rising, position an oven rack in the center of the oven and preheat the oven to 450°F (230°C).

When the dough is ready, uncover it and dimple down any areas that look like they need it. Scatter the whole sage leaves evenly over the top. Drizzle the surface with the remaining 2 tablespoons oil and season with the coarse salt and pepper.

Bake the focaccia until the top is crispy and golden brown and the onions are golden with a few blackened spots here and there, 20–25 minutes. With a large offset spatula, gently lift the focaccia out of the pan and slide it onto a wire rack to cool for at least 20 minutes. Serve warm or at room temperature, cut into rectangles.

Piadine with Prosciutto, Mozzarella, and Arugula

Piadine are soft flatbreads from Emilia-Romagna that are typically topped with prosciutto and a local soft, tangy cheese called squacquerone and then folded over and enjoyed warm (I've substituted fresh mozzarella). I rarely use lard in cooking or baking, but for some traditional recipes, it makes a difference, and this is one. The small amount in the dough gives the piadina a rich, redolent aroma and flavor. The filling here is classic, but feel free to get creative: tomatoes, grilled peppers, sausage, and salami are all typical and delicious.

DOUGH

2 ½–2 ¾ cups (315–345 g) unbleached all-purpose flour, plus more for dusting

4 tablespoons (60 g) rendered leaf lard or pork fatback or unsalted butter, cut into 4 pieces, at cool room temperature

½ cup (120 ml) whole milk

½ cup (120 ml) water

1 teaspoon fine sea salt

¾ teaspoon baking powder

FILLING

3 cups (60 g) arugula

1 tablespoon extra-virgin olive oil

½ lb (225 g) thinly sliced prosciutto di Parma (not trimmed of fat)

¾–1 lb (340–450 g) fresh buffalo's or cow's milk mozzarella cheese, thinly sliced

MAKES 6 PIADINE; 6 SERVINGS

To make the dough, mound the flour on a clean work surface and drop the lard into it. Using your fingers, rub the fat into the flour. It doesn't have to be completely or evenly distributed. Gather the mound back together and make a wide well in the center.

Pour the milk and water into a microwave-safe bowl and heat in a microwave on 50 percent power until warm (about 105°F/40°C), 30–60 seconds. Pour the warm liquid into the flour well and add the salt and baking powder. Using a fork, begin to incorporate the flour into the liquid, pulling the flour from the inside wall of the well and mixing until a ragged dough starts to form. Switch to your hands and knead for several minutes until the dough forms a smooth, elastic ball. The dough should be fairly soft but not sticky. Place it on a lightly floured surface, cover with a damp kitchen towel, plastic wrap, or a bowl, and let rest for 1–3 hours.

Lightly flour a sheet pan. Divide the dough into 6 equal pieces. Shape each piece into a ball and place the balls on the prepared sheet pan. Cover again and let rest for 30 minutes. Preheat the oven to 200°F (95°C) just before you are ready to begin shaping the piadine.

Sprinkle the work surface with a little flour. Lay a roughly 12-inch (30-cm) sheet of parchment or waxed paper alongside the work surface. Place a dough ball on the floured surface and roll out into a disk about 10 inches (25 cm) in diameter and ⅛ inch (3 mm) thick. Prick it all over with a fork and place it on the parchment. Repeat with the remaining dough balls, stacking the disks as you go and separating them with parchment or waxed paper.

Place a large nonstick or seasoned cast-iron frying pan over medium heat. Once it is hot (after 1–2 minutes), place a dough disk in the pan and cook until lightly charred in spots on the bottom, 3–4 minutes. Turn it over with a spatula and cook until charred in spots on the second side and cooked through, about 3 minutes. Transfer the piadina to a sheet pan or ovenproof plate and slip it into the oven to keep warm. Cook the remaining disks the same way, transferring them to the oven as you go.

To fill the piadine, in a bowl, toss the arugula with the oil until evenly coated. Layer one-sixth of the arugula, prosciutto, and mozzarella on a warm piadina and fold in half, pressing lightly. Repeat with the remaining piadine and filling ingredients, then serve warm.

COOK'S NOTE
If you find yourself with leftover lard, store it in a tightly lidded jar in the refrigerator or freeze it for longer keeping. Substitute lard for all or a portion of the butter or shortening in your favorite piecrust or biscuit recipe for beautifully flaky results.

MEAT

FISH

Sliced Steak with Cherry Tomato Confit

Tagliata, as sliced steak is known in Italian, is a specialty of Tuscany, where some of Italy's best beef is raised. Here, the steak is grilled and paired with sweet, slow-roasted cherry tomatoes, which add a touch of voluptuousness.

CONFIT

4 cups (680 g) cherry tomatoes (1 1/2 lb)

1 large shallot, thinly sliced

1/2 cup (120 ml) extra-virgin olive oil

1 teaspoon minced fresh rosemary

1/2–3/4 teaspoon red pepper flakes

1 teaspoon fine sea salt

STEAKS

2 boneless rib-eye or New York strip steaks, each 1 1/2–1 3/4 inches (4–4.5 cm) thick and nicely marbled

1 tablespoon extra-virgin olive oil

Generous pinch of fine sea salt

Freshly ground black pepper

1 fresh rosemary sprig, for garnish

MAKES 4 SERVINGS

COOK'S NOTE

This confit is best when the tomatoes are cooked slowly, so they poach in the oil. To speed up the process, raise the oven temperature to 325°F (165°C) and cook for about 1 hour.

To make the confit, preheat the oven to 275°F (135°C). In a bowl, combine the tomatoes, shallot, oil, rosemary, red pepper flakes to taste, and salt and toss with a rubber spatula to coat the tomatoes and shallot with the oil and aromatics. Scrape the mixture into a baking dish and spread in an even layer.

Bake, stirring occasionally, for 2 hours. The confit is ready when most of the tomatoes have collapsed and released some of their juices and a few of them are still wholly round but softened. If they don't seem quite finished, bake for up to 30 minutes longer (see Cook's Note). Remove from the oven and cover to keep warm.

To prepare the steaks, remove them from the refrigerator about 30 minutes ahead of cooking. Rub them on both sides with the oil and season them on both sides and the edges with the salt and a couple of grindings of pepper. Let stand at room temperature for 15–30 minutes.

Prepare a charcoal grill or gas grill for direct grilling over high heat (450°–500°F/230°–260°C).

Brush the grill grates clean.

Place the steaks directly over the fire, close the lid, and grill for 3 minutes. Turn the steaks, close the lid again, and grill for 3 minutes longer, or until an instant-read thermometer inserted into the center of a steak registers 120°F (49°C) for rare or 125°F (52°C) for medium-rare. If not done, close the lid again and grill for another 2 minutes. Transfer the steaks to a cutting board and let rest for 5 minutes.

To serve, cut the steaks across the grain into thin slices and arrange on a platter. Drizzle just a little of the juice from the tomato confit over the steaks and arrange a few of the whole tomatoes and the rosemary sprig on the platter. Spoon the rest of the confit into a bowl and serve on the side.

Chicken Ricotta Meatballs in Tomato Sauce

These tender meatballs are a nice change from the classic version made with pork and beef. Toss with spaghetti, spoon over polenta, or serve as is, with salad and bread on the side. They also make fantastic leftovers.

MEATBALLS

1 lb (450 g) boneless, skinless chicken breasts, chopped

1 cup (225 g) whole-milk ricotta cheese, well drained (see Cook's Note, page 79)

1 cup (40 g) fresh bread crumbs

½ cup (60 g) freshly grated Parmigiano Reggiano cheese, plus more for serving

1 clove garlic, finely grated

2 tablespoons finely chopped fresh flat-leaf parsley

Finely grated zest of 1 lemon

1 large egg, lightly beaten

½ teaspoon fine sea salt

3 tablespoons extra-virgin olive oil

SAUCE

¼ cup (60 ml) extra-virgin olive oil

½ yellow onion, finely chopped

1 small dried chile, or pinch of red pepper flakes

2 bottles (24 oz/680 g each) tomato passata (purée) or

2 cans (28 oz/800 g each) whole tomatoes, passed through a food mill fitted with finest-hole disk

1 small carrot, peeled

1 large fresh basil sprig, plus 4 or 5 whole leaves

Fine sea salt

MAKES 6 SERVINGS

To make the meatballs, put the chicken breasts into a food processor and pulse about fifty times until finely minced. Scrape the chicken into a large bowl and add the ricotta, bread crumbs, cheese, garlic, parsley, lemon zest, egg, and salt. Stir everything together with a sturdy spoon until thoroughly combined.

Line a large plate with waxed paper. Dampen your hands lightly with cold water and roll the chicken mixture into smallish balls about the size of a walnut, setting them on the waxed paper–lined plate as you go. You should end up with 24 balls. Place in the refrigerator to chill while you make the sauce.

To make the sauce, in a heavy-bottomed saucepan over medium-low heat, combine the oil, onion, and chile and cook, stirring, until the onion is softened and barely golden, about 7 minutes. Stir in the passata (watch for spatters), add the carrot and basil sprig, and season with a pinch of salt. Raise the heat to medium and bring to a boil, then reduce the heat to medium-low and cook, stirring occasionally, until somewhat reduced, 20–30 minutes.

While the sauce is cooking, begin cooking the meatballs. In a large frying pan over medium heat, warm the oil. Add as many meatballs as will fit without crowding and cook, turning them as needed, until browned on all sides, 8–10 minutes. Using a slotted spatula or spoon, transfer them to the sauce. Brown the remaining meatballs the same way, then transfer them to the sauce.

Cover partially and cook until the meatballs have absorbed some of the sauce and the sauce is thickened and richly flavored, 15–20 minutes.

Remove and discard the carrot and the basil sprig and stir in the whole basil leaves. Spoon the meatballs and sauce into shallow bowls, top each bowl with a little Parmigiano, and serve.

Pork Pot Roast with Bay Leaf

The Italian word for pot roast is stracotto, which translates to "overcooked." It may not sound appetizing, but it's exactly what we're going for here. The roast braises slowly in a sauce of vegetables, wine, and herbs, absorbing all the flavors and turning meltingly tender. Use high-quality heritage pork, if possible, as the meat is richer and less dry than mass-produced pork.

1 tablespoon sunflower or other neutral oil

1 bone-in pork shoulder roast, 2 ½–3 lb (1.1–1.4 kg)

Fine sea salt and freshly ground black pepper

4 carrots, peeled and cut into small dice

2 celery ribs with leafy tops, finely chopped

1 yellow onion, finely chopped

1 clove garlic, lightly crushed

3 tablespoons minced fresh flat-leaf parsley

1 fresh bay leaf

3–4 fresh thyme sprigs

¾ cup (180 ml) dry white wine

¾ cup (180 ml) chicken broth or water

MAKES 4 SERVINGS

Preheat the oven to 325°F (165°C).

In a Dutch oven or other heavy-bottomed pot that will hold the roast snugly, add the oil and place over medium-high heat. Lightly season the pork on both sides with salt and pepper and put it into the pot. Brown until nicely seared on the bottom, about 4 minutes, then turn and brown the other side, about 4 minutes longer. Transfer the roast to a plate.

Reduce the heat to low and stir in the carrots, celery, onion, garlic, and 2 tablespoons of the parsley. Cook, stirring often, until the vegetables have started to soften and turn translucent, about 10 minutes. Add the bay leaf and thyme sprigs, raise the heat to medium-high, and stir in the wine. Let the wine bubble briefly, then stir in the broth. Return the meat to the pot and bring the liquid to a boil.

Cover the pot and transfer it to the oven. Braise the roast, turning it every 45 minutes or so, until the meat is silky and a fork easily slides through it, 2–2 ½ hours.

Transfer the roast to a cutting board and cover to keep warm. If necessary, set the pot on the stove top over low heat to reduce the sauce until nicely thickened. Remove and discard the bay leaf and thyme sprigs. The sauce can be served as is or puréed with an immersion blender.

Slice the roast or separate it into chunks, then arrange on a platter. Spoon the sauce on top, garnish with the remaining 1 tablespoon parsley, and serve.

Sausage, Peppers, and Potatoes

This stove-top stew of sorts is the perfect weeknight dinner. Everything is cooked in the same pan, and it all comes together in less than an hour. I like to serve it in September, when peppers are at their best, with grilled bread on the side.

1 lb (450 g) spicy or sweet Italian sausages (about 4 links; I use 2 sweet and 2 spicy)

3 tablespoons extra-virgin olive oil, plus more for serving

1 large sweet onion, such as Maui, Vidalia, or Walla Walla, cut into thin wedges

2 red bell peppers, halved lengthwise, seeded, and cut lengthwise into narrow slices

1 fresh bay leaf

½ teaspoon fine sea salt

Pinch of red pepper flakes (optional)

2 yellow potatoes, peeled and cut into 1-inch (2.5-cm) chunks

1 cup (240 g) tomato passata (purée)

¼ cup (60 ml) water

4 thick slices coarse country bread, grilled or toasted (optional)

MAKES 4 SERVINGS

Cut the sausages in half crosswise. In a large frying pan or sauté pan over medium-high heat, warm 1 tablespoon of the oil. Arrange the sausages in the pan and cook, turning as needed, until browned all over, about 10 minutes. Transfer the sausages to a plate.

Reduce the heat to medium-low and add the remaining 2 tablespoons oil. Add the onion, bell peppers, bay leaf, salt, and red pepper flakes (if using) and cook, stirring often, until the vegetables are somewhat softened, 10–12 minutes. Tip in the potatoes and cook, stirring from time to time, until the potatoes start to soften, 10–15 minutes longer.

Pour in the tomato passata and water and mix well. Return the sausages to the pan, raise the heat to medium-high, and bring to a simmer. Reduce the heat to medium-low, cover partially, and simmer gently until all the vegetables are completely tender, about 30 minutes. The dish is done when you can easily crush a piece of potato against the side of the pan with a wooden spoon.

Spoon the stew into shallow bowls and tuck a slice of grilled bread, if using, into each bowl. Drizzle a thread of olive oil on top of each bowl and serve.

Grilled Lamb Loin Chops with Grilled Peppers

For centuries, sheep farming was a way of life in Abruzzo, the mountainous region that extends east of Rome from the Apennines to the Adriatic Sea. For some, it still is. Abruzzo is known for its excellent sheep's milk cheeses and for its high-quality lamb. The meat is often grilled, with just salt and pepper to season it. Sweet bell peppers on the side deliver an assertive punch of flavor and cut through the lamb's richness.

8 lamb loin chops, each about 1 inch (2.5 cm) thick

4 red bell peppers

Extra-virgin olive oil, for grilling the peppers and lamb

Fine sea salt

1 tablespoon aged balsamic vinegar

Freshly ground black pepper

Best-quality extra-virgin olive oil, for drizzling

1 small handful fresh herb sprigs, such as rosemary or oregano

MAKES 4–6 SERVINGS

Prepare a gas grill for direct grilling over medium heat (375°–400°F/190°–200°C). If using a charcoal grill, create two fire zones, one at medium heat and one at medium-high heat (475°–500°F/250°–260°C). Remove the lamb chops from the refrigerator 20–30 minutes before grilling.

Brush the grill grates clean. Halve the peppers lengthwise and seed them. Turn them skin side down, then brush the insides lightly with oil and sprinkle with salt. Place the peppers, cut side down, over direct medium heat on the grill and close the lid. Grill, turning occasionally, until lightly charred in places and somewhat softened. Transfer them to a serving plate and drizzle with the balsamic vinegar and a glug or two of your best olive oil. Season with a pinch of salt and a few grindings of pepper and arrange a few herb sprigs on top. Let the peppers rest while you grill the lamb.

If using a gas grill, raise the heat to medium-high (475°–500°F/250°–260°C).

Rub 2 tablespoons oil into all sides of the lamb chops. Season the chops generously with salt and pepper on all sides. Place the chops on the grill over direct medium-high heat, close the lid, and grill for 4 minutes. Turn the chops, close the lid again, and grill for 5 minutes longer, or until an instant-read thermometer inserted into the center of a chop away from bone registers 125°F (52°C) for medium-rare. Transfer the chops to a plate or cutting board and let rest for 5 minutes.

Arrange the lamb chops on the platter alongside the peppers. Scatter a few herb sprigs on top and serve.

Short Rib Bollito with Salsa Verde

Whenever I make homemade beef broth, I always save the cooked meat and carrots and serve them drizzled with good olive oil and garnished with a spoonful of piquant salsa verde. *This dish, in which short ribs create a savory broth as they gently poach in an herb-spiked liquid, is sort of a simplified version.*

BOLLITO

2 ½–3 lb (1.1–1.4 kg) meaty beef short ribs

Fine sea salt and freshly ground black pepper

2 large or 4 medium carrots, peeled and cut into 3-inch (7.5-cm) lengths

1 large celery rib, cut into 3-inch (7.5-cm) lengths

1 yellow onion, quartered

3 fresh bay leaves

3 fresh flat-leaf parsley sprigs, plus 4 more for garnish

SALSA VERDE

4 cups (60 g) lightly packed fresh flat-leaf parsley leaves

2 anchovy fillets in olive oil (I like Rizzoli alici in salsa picante)

1 clove garlic, cut into pieces

½ cup (20 g) fresh bread crumbs

1 tablespoon capers, rinsed and patted dry

Fine sea salt and freshly ground black pepper

1 tablespoon red wine vinegar

½ cup (120 ml) extra-virgin olive oil, plus more if needed

MAKES 4 SERVINGS

To make the bollito, season the short ribs on both sides with salt and pepper. Arrange them in a single layer in a Dutch oven or other heavy-bottomed pot and add the carrots, celery, onion, bay leaves, and 3 parsley sprigs. Pour in water to cover the meat by 1 inch (2.5 cm) and set over medium heat. Bring to a boil, skimming any foam that forms on the surface. Reduce the heat to medium-low or low to maintain a gentle simmer, cover, and cook until the meat is completely tender and a fork slides through it easily, 2 ½–3 hours. Taste the broth toward the end of cooking and adjust the seasoning with salt if needed. Remove from the heat and let rest, covered, for 10 minutes.

While the bollito is cooking, make the salsa verde. In a food processor, combine the parsley, anchovies, garlic, bread crumbs, capers, ½ teaspoon salt, and a grinding of pepper and pulse briefly to chop the ingredients roughly. Sprinkle in the vinegar and pulse again briefly to mix. With the motor running, drizzle in the oil and process until you have a smooth, creamy sauce. Add a drop or two more oil if needed to achieve a good consistency. Scrape the sauce into a bowl, cover, and set aside.

Spoon the short ribs into shallow bowls along with a few spoonfuls of the cooking liquid. Garnish each serving with a couple of pieces of cooked carrot, a parsley sprig, and a dollop of salsa verde, and serve, passing the remaining salsa verde at the table.

Livorno-Style Cod with Olives and Capers

I love the port city of Livorno, on the coast of Tuscany, for two reasons: it's the birthplace of Amadeo Modigliani, one of my favorite Italian artists, and it's where you'll find some of the best seafood dishes on the Mediterranean coast, including this classic preparation.

3 tablespoons extra-virgin olive oil, plus more for serving

2 cloves garlic, lightly crushed

1½ lb (680 g) skin-on cod loin, cut into 4 equal pieces

Fine sea salt and freshly ground black pepper

⅓ cup (80 ml) dry white wine

⅓ cup (50 g) packed pitted salt-cured olives, halved

1 tablespoon nonpareil capers, rinsed and patted dry

3 tablespoons finely chopped fresh flat-leaf parsley

Pinch of red pepper flakes

⅔ cup (135 g) diced canned tomatoes

MAKES 4 SERVINGS

In a large frying pan over medium-low heat, warm the oil and garlic for about 2 minutes, pressing down on the garlic to release its fragrance. Season the cod lightly with salt and pepper and arrange the pieces, skin side down, in the pan. Cook for 3 minutes, then pour in the wine and let it bubble for a minute or so. Add the olives, capers, 2 tablespoons of the parsley, the red pepper flakes, and tomatoes and bring to a simmer. Reduce the heat to low, cover partially, and cook until the fish is opaque, 6–8 minutes. Uncover and cook until the liquid is reduced and thickened to a sauce, 2–3 minutes longer.

Transfer the fish and sauce to individual plates. Top each serving with the remaining 1 tablespoon parsley, dividing it evenly, and a drizzle of oil, and serve.

Adriatic Seafood Stew

Variations of this hearty stew abound all along Italy's Adriatic coast, from Trieste in the northern region of Friuli down to Puglia on the southeastern tip. Each regional version is slightly different, depending on the local catch. In Abruzzo, where my family is from, the stew is spiked with chile and served with grilled or toasted bread to soak up the rich sauce.

3 tablespoons extra-virgin olive oil

2 cloves garlic, lightly crushed

1 small yellow onion, finely diced

1 celery rib, finely diced

2 tablespoons finely chopped fresh flat-leaf parsley

½ teaspoon red pepper flakes

½ cup (120 ml) dry white wine

2 fresh oregano sprigs, plus 4 more garnish

2 fresh bay leaves

2–3 cups (475–700 ml) fish or seafood stock (see Cook's Note)

1 cup (200 g) finely chopped or crushed canned tomatoes

12 littleneck clams, well rinsed and scrubbed

12 mussels, well rinsed, scrubbed, and debearded

8 large head-on tiger shrimp, or 16 shell-on jumbo shrimp

1 lb (450 g) meaty white fish fillet, such as cod, monkfish, or snapper or a mix, cut into 2-inch (5-cm) pieces

2 tablespoons fresh lemon juice

FOR SERVING

8 baguette slices

1 clove garlic, lightly crushed

Extra-virgin olive oil

4 fresh oregano sprigs

MAKES 4 SERVINGS

In a large Dutch oven or other heavy-bottomed pot, combine the oil, garlic, onion, celery, parsley, and the red pepper flakes to taste. Set over medium-low heat and cook, stirring from time to time, until the onion and celery are tender, 15–20 minutes. Raise the heat to medium-high, stir in the wine, and let it bubble until some of it is absorbed, 1–2 minutes. Toss in the 2 oregano sprigs and the bay leaves. Stir in 2 cups (475 ml) of the stock and the tomatoes and bring to a boil. Reduce the heat to medium-low and simmer gently, uncovered, until slightly thickened, about 20 minutes.

Arrange the clams and mussels in the pot (discarding any that failed to close to the touch), cover, and simmer for 5 minutes. Uncover and add the shrimp and fish, spooning some of the sauce on top. Add more stock if needed to loosen the sauce. Re-cover and cook at a gentle simmer until the clams and mussels open and the shrimp and fish are cooked through, 5–10 minutes. Remove from the heat and stir in the lemon juice.

While the stew is cooking, prepare the ingredients for serving. Preheat the broiler. Arrange the baguette slices on a sheet pan and broil until nicely browned and slightly charred on the edges, 1–2 minutes. Rub the slices with the garlic while still warm.

Spoon the stew into 4 shallow rimmed bowls, dividing the fish and shellfish evenly among them (discard any clams or mussels that failed to open). Tuck 2 baguette slices into each bowl. Drizzle 1 tablespoon oil onto each serving, then garnish each bowl with an oregano sprig and serve.

COOK'S NOTE
If you don't have a favorite fish or seafood stock, check your local fish shop and supermarket seafood department, which often carry stock. You can also substitute bottled clam juice for the stock.

Neapolitan-Style Mussels and Clams

Mussels and clams often come together in Neapolitan dishes, and this aromatic stew is a classic example. It's easy to make and is delicious with grilled country bread. Serve with a simple insalata mista *and a crisp white wine for a light meal.*

2 lb (1 kg) mussels

2 lb (1 kg) clams

6 tablespoons (90 ml) extra-virgin olive oil

2 cloves garlic, lightly crushed

1 fresh red chile, minced, or generous pinch of red pepper flakes

1 can (28 oz/800 g) whole tomatoes with juices

4 tablespoons (8 g) finely chopped fresh flat-leaf parsley

⅓ cup (80 ml) dry white wine

4–6 slices coarse country bread

MAKES 4–6 SERVINGS

Rinse the mussels and clams in several changes of cold water and scrub them clean, removing any beards from the mussels. Discard any that fail to close to the touch.

Film a large, heavy-bottomed saucepan with 4 tablespoons (60 ml) of the oil. Add 1 of the garlic cloves and the chile, and set the pan on the stove top. Turn on the heat to medium-low and cook for about 2 minutes, pressing down on the garlic to release its fragrance.

Break up the tomatoes with your hands or a pair of kitchen scissors and add them to the oil (watch for spatters). Stir in 3 tablespoons of the parsley, raise the heat to medium-high, and bring to a boil. Lower the heat to a gentle simmer and cook, stirring occasionally, until the tomatoes are just starting to break down, about 10 minutes. Reduce the heat to its lowest setting and cover to keep warm.

In a separate large saucepan over medium-low heat, warm the remaining 2 tablespoons oil and 1 garlic clove, pressing down on the garlic to release its fragrance. When the oil is hot, slide the shellfish into the pan and stir briefly to coat with the oil. Raise the heat to medium-high and cover. When the shellfish is hot, uncover and cook, stirring, for a minute or two until the shellfish starts to sizzle. Then pour in the wine and stir. Re-cover the pan and cook for 5 minutes. Uncover the pan and use tongs to transfer the mussels and clams that have opened to the pan of sauce. Re-cover the pan and let the unopened shellfish cook until they open, which should take just a few minutes longer. The clams and mussels should take no more than 10 minutes total to open. Transfer the opened shellfish to the sauce and discard any that failed to open.

Line a fine-mesh sieve with a damp paper towel and pour the liquid remaining in the shellfish pan through the sieve into a small bowl. Pour the filtered liquid into the pan with the shellfish and sauce, stir everything together, cover, and reduce the heat to medium-low. Cook, stirring once or twice, until heated through, about 6 minutes.

When the shellfish is almost ready, preheat the broiler. Arrange the bread slices on a sheet pan and broil until nicely browned and charred around the edges, 2–3 minutes.

Spoon the shellfish and sauce into individual bowls and tuck a slice of bread into each bowl. Sprinkle the remaining parsley on top and serve.

COOK'S NOTE
As you might expect, this stew goes particularly well with wines from Campania, the region that includes Naples. Two of my favorites are Greco di Tufo, a full-bodied white with hints of acidity, and Fiano di Avellino, straw-yellow in color and fruity in flavor, with notes of almond and spice.

Grilled Shrimp with Orzo

Warm orzo pasta tossed with peas, fresh herbs, and a simple lemon dressing makes a soft, savory bed for grilled shrimp. For the herbs, I like mint and oregano and just a little marjoram for a floral note, but feel free to use your own favorite mix. Steamed fresh asparagus cut into bite-size pieces is a nice springtime substitute for the peas.

SHRIMP

2 tablespoons extra-virgin olive oil

Pinch of red pepper flakes

24 jumbo shrimp, peeled with tail segments intact and deveined

Pinch of fine sea salt

ORZO

⅓ cup (80 ml) fresh lemon juice

2 teaspoons finely grated lemon zest

⅓ cup (80 ml) extra-virgin olive oil

Fine sea salt

1½ cups (300 g) regular or whole-wheat orzo

Freshly ground black pepper

2 red or white spring onions, bulb and pale green stems, thinly sliced

1½ cups (210 g) frozen peas, thawed

2 tablespoons chopped mixed fresh herbs, such as marjoram, mint, and oregano, plus sprigs for garnish

½ cup (60 g) freshly grated Parmigiano Reggiano cheese

MAKES 4–6 SERVINGS

To make the shrimp, soak 6 wooden skewers in cold water for 30 minutes. In a small bowl, stir together the oil and red pepper flakes. When the skewers are done soaking, pat them dry and thread 4 shrimp onto each skewer, passing the skewer through the head end and tail end of each shrimp. Brush both sides of the loaded skewers with the spicy oil and sprinkle lightly with salt. Prepare a charcoal grill or gas grill for direct grilling over medium heat (400°F/200°C).

While the grill is heating, make the orzo. In a small bowl, whisk together the lemon juice and zest, oil, and 1 teaspoon salt to make a dressing and set aside. Bring a saucepan of water to a rolling boil and salt generously. Pour in the orzo and cook, stirring occasionally to prevent sticking, until al dente, according to package instructions. Drain well, then transfer the orzo to a bowl. Add three-fourths of the dressing and toss gently to combine, then season with a generous grinding of pepper. Fold in the onions, peas, chopped herbs, and cheese, mixing well. Fold in the remaining dressing, then taste and adjust with salt and pepper if needed. Spoon onto a platter and cover to keep warm.

Brush the grill grates clean. Arrange the skewers directly over the fire and grill (with the lid closed if using a gas grill), turning them once at the midpoint, until the shrimp turn pink and are opaque throughout, 6–8 minutes.

Slide the shrimp off of the skewers and arrange them on top of the orzo. Garnish with the herb sprigs and serve.

VEGETABLES

EGGS

Eggplant Involtini with Mozzarella

My friend Carla Tomasi is a retired chef turned cooking teacher who lives in Rome. A few years ago, she invited me to sit in on one of her classes in which she made this classic southern Italian dish of silky eggplant slices rolled around a filling of stretchy cheese and baked in tomato sauce. Many recipes call for frying the eggplant, but Carla bakes hers, and it makes for a lighter and more appetizing result—summer comfort food at its best. Serve this as a side dish or vegetarian main course.

SAUCE

3 tablespoons extra-virgin olive oil

1 clove garlic, lightly crushed

1 bottle (24 oz/680 g) tomato passata (purée), or 1 can (28 oz/800 g) whole tomatoes, passed through a food mill fitted with the finest-hole disk

½ teaspoon fine sea salt

4 fresh basil leaves, torn

INVOLTINI

2 large eggplants, 2 lb (1 kg) total weight

Fine sea salt

Extra-virgin olive oil, for the eggplant and the baking dish

¼ lb (115 g) fresh mozzarella cheese

¼ lb (115 g) scamorza or additional fresh mozzarella cheese

¼ lb (115 g) semi-aged pecorino, Asiago fresco, or other good Italian melty cheese

1 cup (115 g) freshly grated Parmigiano Reggiano cheese

MAKES 4–8 SERVINGS

To make the sauce, in a saucepan or large, deep frying pan, combine the oil and garlic over medium heat and cook for about 2 minutes, pressing down on the garlic to release its flavor. Pour in the tomato passata (watch for spatters) and season with the salt. Raise the heat to medium-high, bring to a simmer, and cook uncovered, stirring from time to time, until the oil pools on the surface and the sauce is nicely thickened, 25–30 minutes. Stir in the basil and remove from the heat.

While the sauce is cooking, begin preparing the involtini. Line a large sheet pan with paper towels. Trim off the ends of the eggplants and cut them lengthwise into slices ¼ inch (6 mm) thick. You should have 8 slices from each eggplant for a total of 16 slices. Salt the eggplant slices on both sides and lay them on the towel-lined sheet pan. Let sit for 1 hour, then pat them dry.

Preheat the oven to 400°F (200°C). Line 2 sheet pans with parchment paper. Brush the eggplant slices on both sides with oil and arrange 8 slices in a single layer on each prepared sheet pan. Bake for 10 minutes, then turn the slices and bake until they are tender and lightly browned, about 10 minutes longer. (You can bake them 1 sheet pan at a time, or both sheet pans at once on racks placed in the top third and center of the oven.) Let the slices cool while you prepare the filling. Reduce the oven temperature to 375°F (190°C).

Cut the mozzarella and scamorza into small cubes and transfer to a bowl. Shred the pecorino on the large holes of a box grater and add to the bowl, then stir in the Parmigiano.

Lightly coat an 8 x 11-inch (22 x 28-cm) baking dish with 1 tablespoon oil. Spoon about ⅓ cup (80 ml) of the sauce onto the bottom of the dish. Set aside about ½ cup (60 g) of the cheese mixture to use for topping. Place a spoonful of the cheese mixture on the wide end of an eggplant slice, roll up the eggplant, and set the roll, seam side down, in the baking dish. Fill and roll the remaining eggplant slices the same way and place them, seam side down, in the dish. The rolls should fit snugly in the dish. Spoon the remaining tomato sauce over the rolls and top evenly with the remaining cheese.

Bake uncovered until the filling is oozy and the top is browned in spots, 30–40 minutes. Let sit for at least 5 minutes before serving. Serve hot or warm.

COOK'S NOTE

When choosing eggplant, look for fruit that is smooth and shiny with no scuffs or bruises. It should be firm but not hard, with a green (not brown) stem, and it should feel heavy. If the eggplant feels light, chances are its old, and it's flesh will be pithy and bitter.

Honey-Roasted Carrots with Balsamic Vinegar

Carrots are the workhorse of the vegetable world. Many cooks have a bag of carrots in their fridge, but mostly they use them as an afterthought, something to dip into a bowl of hummus or to chop up finely and add to a soup or stew. I love recipes like this one that showcase the carrot's attributes—its vibrant color, its sweet, earthy flavor, and its tender bite.

1 lb (450 g) young carrots

3 tablespoons extra-virgin olive oil

1 tablespoon runny honey

Fine sea salt and freshly ground black pepper

2–3 teaspoons aged balsamic vinegar

2 teaspoons finely chopped fresh flat-leaf parsley

MAKES 4 SERVINGS

Preheat the oven to 400°F (200°C). Line a sheet pan with aluminum foil. Peel the carrots. If they are very small, cut them in half lengthwise. Otherwise, cut them in half crosswise, then cut each half lengthwise into quarters to make slim batons. Pile the carrots onto the prepared sheet pan.

In a small bowl, whisk together the oil and honey. Pour the oil-honey mixture over the carrots and toss to coat evenly. Spread the carrots in a single layer on the pan and season with ½ teaspoon salt and a grinding of pepper. Roast for 10 minutes; toss and continue to roast until just tender, 5–10 minutes more. Remove from the oven.

Position an oven rack in the top third of the oven and turn the oven to broil. Slide the carrots under the broiler and broil until lightly charred in spots, 2–3 minutes.

Spoon the carrots onto a platter and drizzle the vinegar evenly over the top. Sprinkle with salt and the parsley and serve.

Potato and Eggplant Frittata

Some of the best dishes I've made started as leftovers. This frittata was an excuse to use up leftover grilled eggplant. My family and I enjoyed it so much that we have put it into regular rotation during the summer when it's easy to find young eggplants with few seeds.

1 long, thin eggplant or 2 small eggplants, about ½ lb (225 g) total weight

Extra-virgin olive oil

Fine sea salt and freshly ground black pepper

½ red onion, finely chopped

1 yellow potato, cut into ¾-inch (2-cm) cubes

1 tablespoon finely chopped mixed fresh herbs, such as marjoram, mint, oregano, flat-leaf parsley, and thyme

5 large eggs

¼ cup (30 g) freshly grated Parmigiano Reggiano cheese

¼ cup (60 g) shredded ricotta salata or smoked ricotta cheese, cut into ½-inch (1-cm) cubes

MAKES 4 SERVINGS

Preheat the broiler, or prepare a charcoal grill or gas grill for direct grilling over high heat (450°–500°F/230°–260°C) and brush the grill grates clean.

Trim off the ends of the eggplant and cut crosswise into slices ½ inch (12 mm) thick. Brush the slices on both sides with oil and season lightly with salt and pepper.

Arrange the slices on a sheet pan and slip under the broiler, or place the slices directly over the fire on the grill. Cook, turning two or three times, until lightly charred on both sides and tender, about 10 minutes. Transfer to a plate and set aside.

In a frying pan over medium heat, combine 3 tablespoons oil and the onion and cook, stirring, until the onion is just starting to soften, about 5 minutes. Stir in the potato cubes, coating them with the oil. Cook, stirring often to prevent the potato cubes from sticking, until just tender, about 15 minutes. Sprinkle in the herbs and remove from the heat.

Preheat the broiler. Coat the bottom and sides of a 9-inch (23-cm) cast-iron or ovenproof nonstick frying pan with 2 tablespoons oil. In a bowl, beat together the eggs, ½ teaspoon salt, and the Parmigiano until blended. Pour three-fourths of the egg mixture into the prepared frying pan. Spread the potatoes over the eggs and scatter the ricotta evenly on top. Press the eggplant slices into the eggs, covering the surface completely. Pour the remaining egg mixture evenly on top. Place over medium-low heat and cook until the bottom is set and nicely browned and the top is nearly set, about 8 minutes.

Slide the frittata under the broiler and broil until set and browned on top, 2–4 minutes. Let rest for about 1 minute, then transfer the frittata to a serving plate. Serve hot or warm. (Leftovers are great cold.)

Rice-Stuffed Tomatoes

This one takes me right back to summers at the beach in Italy, when my mom would make stuffed vegetables for pranzo (lunch). She used a mix of summer vegetables (zucchini, peppers, onions, tomatoes) and a variety of fillings (bread, meat, rice), but she always stuffed the tomatoes with rice. This dish is meant to be served at room temperature, as so many Italian dishes are in summer. It makes them all the more appetizing.

3 cups (700 ml) water

Fine sea salt

1½ cups (300 g) Arborio rice

2 lb (1 kg) Yukon gold potatoes

¼ cup (60 ml) extra-virgin olive oil, plus more for the baking dish and drizzling

12 ripe medium tomatoes

1 ball (½ lb/225 g) fresh mozzarella cheese, cut into cubes

½ cup (60 g) freshly grated Parmigiano Reggiano cheese

2 tablespoons minced fresh flat-leaf parsley

2 tablespoons chopped fresh basil, plus a few whole leaves for garnish

2 teaspoons minced fresh oregano

Freshly ground black pepper

2 teaspoons minced fresh rosemary

MAKES 6 OR MORE SERVINGS

In a saucepan, bring the water to a boil over high heat and salt moderately. Pour in the rice, cover, reduce the heat to a gentle simmer, and cook until the rice is slightly undercooked and most of the liquid is absorbed, about 17 minutes. Drain the rice and pour it into a bowl to cool.

While the rice is cooking, cook the potatoes. In a large pot, combine the potatoes with water to cover. Salt the water generously, bring to a boil over medium-high heat, and boil the potatoes until barely cooked through, 10–12 minutes. To test, poke them with a paring knife; it should meet some resistance. Drain and let cool.

Preheat the oven to 400°F (200°C). Select a baking dish just large enough to fit the tomatoes and coat the bottom and sides of it with oil.

Cut a thin slice off the top of each tomato to create a lid. Set a fine-mesh sieve over a bowl and scoop out the insides of the tomatoes, leaving a wall about ¼ inch (6 mm) thick. (I use a melon baller, but a spoon or small knife will also work. Just be sure not to pierce the wall.) Set the tomatoes aside. Using the back of a spoon, press against the pulp and seeds to release as much tomato juice as possible into the bowl. Discard the solids that remain in the colander.

In a bowl, combine the cooked rice with the juices from the tomatoes. Stir in the mozzarella and Parmigiano, parsley, chopped basil, and oregano. Season with a little salt and pepper, then pour in the ¼ cup (60 ml) oil and mix everything together well. Peel the cooled potatoes and slice about ¼ inch (6 mm) thick.

Recipe continues

Rice-Stuffed Tomatoes continued

COOK'S NOTE
If there is rice mixture left over after stuffing the tomatoes, put it into an oiled baking dish just large enough to hold it, cover with foil, and bake alongside the tomatoes for 15 minutes. Uncover and continue to bake until heated through and lightly browned on top, about 15 minutes more.

Arrange a layer of the potato slices, without overlapping, in the bottom of the prepared baking dish. Set the tomatoes, hollow side up, on top of the potatoes. Spoon the rice mixture into the tomatoes, filling each to the top without overstuffing. Place each lid on top of its tomato. Snuggle the remaining potatoes around the tomatoes and around the edge of the baking dish. The dish should be tightly packed. Sprinkle the rosemary over the tomatoes and potatoes and season with a little more salt. Drizzle everything well with oil.

Cover the baking dish with aluminum foil and bake for 35 minutes. Uncover and continue to bake until the tomatoes are nicely browned on top, about 30 minutes more. Remove from the oven and let cool until warm or at room temperature. Scatter a few basil leaves over the top and serve. (Leftovers are delicious straight from the fridge.)

Marinated Fried Zucchini

This classic Roman preparation is best made with young, firm zucchini, the kind you find at the farmers' market—or maybe in your own garden—in late spring or early summer. If you make it later in the season with large ones, you may need to salt them so they release some of their liquid. Use a good-quality neutral oil to fry the zucchini (I like sunflower oil). Once you have added the marinade, let the fried zucchini rest for at least a couple of hours at room temperature or up to overnight in the fridge before serving. This is a side dish to serve with grilled sausages or roast chicken.

1 large clove or 2 small cloves garlic, sliced paper-thin

¼ cup (15 g) finely chopped fresh mint or a mix of mint and basil, plus more for garnish

⅓ cup (80 ml) high-quality white wine vinegar

Sunflower or other neutral oil, for frying

1½ lb (680 g) small or medium zucchini (about 6), sliced crosswise about ¼ inch (6 mm) thick

1 teaspoon fine sea salt

Extra-virgin olive oil, for drizzling

MAKES 4 SERVINGS

In a small bowl, stir together the garlic, mint, and vinegar (I use a glass measuring pitcher for this) and set aside.

Line a wire rack or a sheet pan with paper towels and set it near the stove. Pour the sunflower oil to a depth of 1–1½ inches (2.5– 4 cm) into a deep, heavy-bottomed frying pan or saucepan and heat over medium-high heat to 350°F (180°C) on a deep-frying thermometer. Fry the zucchini slices in small batches, using a wire skimmer to turn them and move them around in the oil as they fry, until golden brown, about 2–3 minutes. As each batch is ready, use the wire skimmer to transfer it to the towel-lined rack to drain. When all the zucchini are fried, sprinkle them with the salt.

Transfer the zucchini to a shallow bowl and pour the vinegar marinade over them. Toss gently with a spoon to coat well. Let sit at room temperature for 2 hours to marinate properly. Or cover the bowl and refrigerate overnight. Bring to room temperture before serving.

Just before serving, scatter some mint over the zucchini and drizzle with a thread of olive oil.

Kale Braised in White Wine

This slim, deep green–blue leafy vegetable goes by several names: dinosaur kale, Tuscan kale, lacinato kale, and, in Italian, cavolo nero. *It can be pretty tough raw, but once it's had a leisurely braise in olive oil and wine, it loses its tough edge and takes on an appealing sweetness.*

¼ cup (60 ml) extra-virgin olive oil

3 large cloves garlic, sliced paper-thin

1 lb (450 g) dinosaur (Tuscan) kale (about 2 bunches), trimmed of tough stems, rinsed but not dried, and cut crosswise into strips 1 inch (2.5 cm) wide

1 teaspoon fine sea salt, plus more if needed

1 small fresh chile, minced, or generous pinch of red pepper flakes

¾ cup (180 ml) dry white wine

MAKES 4 SERVINGS

In a large, deep frying pan or sauté pan over medium-low heat, combine the oil and garlic and cook, stirring often, until the garlic is softened but has not taken on color, about 5 minutes. If necessary, reduce the heat to keep the garlic from browning.

Add the kale by the handful, with any water still clinging to its leaves. If it doesn't all fit into the pan, cover the pan and let it wilt for about 2 minutes, then uncover and add the remaining kale, tossing it with tongs or a wooden spoon to coat it with the oil and garlic. Season with the salt and chile and pour in the wine. Raise the heat to medium-high and let the wine bubble for a minute or so, then cover the pan, reduce the heat to medium-low, and simmer gently, turning the kale with tongs now and again, until tender, 15–20 minutes.

Uncover, taste, and adjust the seasoning with salt if needed. Let cook, uncovered, for another 5 minutes or so to slightly reduce the juices, then serve.

Roasted Peppers with Anchovies

Peppers may be a New World vegetable, but to me they are quintessentially Italian. There is nothing like hearing the clatter of silverware and plates as you walk by a trattoria at lunchtime and then, moments later, catching the beguiling, pungent aroma of freshly roasted peppers on the breeze.

4 red bell peppers

1 clove garlic, sliced paper-thin

6–8 anchovy fillets in olive oil
(I like Rizzoli alici in salsa picante)

1 tablespoon nonpareil capers,
drained and patted dry

1 tablespoon finely chopped
flat-leaf parsley

Best-quality extra-virgin olive oil,
for drizzling

MAKES 4–6 SERVINGS

Position an oven rack in the top third of the oven and preheat the broiler, or prepare a charcoal grill or gas grill for direct grilling over high heat (450°–500°F/230°–260°C).

Line a large sheet pan with aluminum foil, set the pepper on it, and slip it under the broiler. Or place the peppers on grill grates directly over the fire. Broil or grill the peppers, turning them with tongs every few minutes, until they are partially blackened and blistered on all sides, about 10–15 minutes total. Transfer the peppers to a bowl and cover with a kitchen towel. Let steam for 10 minutes.

Gently pull off the stems from the peppers and pour out any liquid. Cut them in half lengthwise and scrape away the seeds and membranes. Lay the halves, skin side up, on a cutting board and gently scrape away the charred skins with a paring knife. Cut each half once more so you have 16 fat lobes total.

Place the peppers in a shallow dish and tuck in the garlic slices. Drape the anchovies on top and scatter on the capers and parsley. Drizzle with your best olive oil. Don't skimp. Let marinate for 30–60 minutes before serving.

Colorful Greens and White Beans

The stems of rainbow chard add a splash of color to this side dish. Creamy cannellini beans provide substance, and a squeeze of lemon juice at serving time gives it just the right amount of zing. Serve alongside roast chicken, grilled or sauteed fish, or an omelet.

2 bunches rainbow chard, about 1 lb (450 g) total weight

3 tablespoons extra-virgin olive oil, plus more as needed

2 cloves garlic, lightly crushed

Pinch of red pepper flakes

Fine sea salt

1½ cups (250 g) cooked cannellini beans (see Cook's Note)

Freshly ground black pepper

½ lemon

MAKES 4 SERVINGS

COOK'S NOTE
Canned beans can be used here, but cooking your own cannellini beans will yield the best result. Soak dried beans overnight in water to cover, then cook them using the method for Oven-Braised Beans in Their Broth (page 148) or simmer them gently on the stove top in plenty of water. You will need ½ cup (100 g) dried beans to yield the 1½ cups (250 g) cooked beans for this recipe. Drain the cooked beans before adding them to the pan of greens.

Trim the ends off the chard stems, then cut the stems from the leaves. Cut the stems into ¾-inch (2-cm) pieces. Stack the leaves, a few at a time, and cut them crosswise into ribbons 1 inch (2.5 cm) wide. Set the stems and leaves aside separately.

Film a large frying pan with 2 tablespoons of the oil. Add 1 of the garlic cloves and set the pan over medium heat. Sprinkle in half of the red pepper flakes and cook for 2 minutes, pressing down on the garlic to release its flavor. Add the chard stems to the pan, tossing them with the oil. Cook, stirring often, until the stems are just tender, 5–7 minutes. They should retain a little bite. Scoop them into a bowl and set aside.

Pour the remaining 1 tablespoon oil into the pan and add the remaining garlic clove and red pepper flakes. Cook for 2 minutes, then add the chard leaves by the handful. If they don't all fit, cover the pan and let them wilt for about 2 minutes, then uncover and add the remaining leaves. When all of the chard leaves are wilted, season with ½ teaspoon salt and cook uncovered, stirring occasionally, until they are tender and have darkened a shade or two, about 15 minutes.

Spoon the cannellini beans into the frying pan and cook, stirring often, until heated through. Add a splash more oil if necessary to prevent sticking. Return the stems to the pan and cook, stirring, until warmed through. Season with a generous grinding of black pepper, then taste and season with more salt if needed and toss everything together.

Transfer to a serving bowl and squeeze the lemon half over the top. Drizzle with a final thread of oil, if you like, and serve warm.

Oven-Braised Beans in Their Broth

If you've never braised beans in the oven, give it a try. Seasoned with woodsy herbs and garlic, they perfume the entire house as they cook, turning tender while still holding their shape. Beans cooked in this way have plenty of uses. They can be the base for pasta e fagioli, *stirred into a country vegetable soup, or puréed and spread on crostini. Or you can keep it simple and serve them warm in their flavorful broth, dressed with excellent olive oil.*

2 cups (400 g) dried cranberry beans, soaked overnight in water to cover

2 fresh sage sprigs

1 fresh rosemary sprig

2 fresh thyme sprigs

2 small cloves garlic, lightly crushed

2 tablespoons extra-virgin olive oil, plus more for drizzling

Fine sea salt and freshly ground black pepper

¼ red onion, thinly sliced

¼ cup (60 ml) red wine vinegar

3 tablespoons water

1 handful fresh flat-leaf parsley leaves

MAKES ABOUT 2 QT (1.9 L) BEANS WITH LIQUID; 8 SERVINGS

Preheat the oven to 350°F (180°C).

Drain the beans and transfer them to a Dutch oven or other heavy-bottomed ovenproof pot with a lid. Tuck in the sage, rosemary, and thyme sprigs and the garlic. Pour in water to cover the beans by 1 inch (2.5 cm). Drizzle the oil over the top. Bring to boil over medium-high heat, then cover the pot and slide it into the oven. Braise the beans at a gentle simmer (check them every so often) until they are tender but still hold their shape, about 2 hours. Toward the end of cooking, stir in about 2 teaspoons salt and a generous grinding of pepper.

While the beans are braising, put the onion into a bowl and stir in the vinegar, water, and a pinch of salt. Let the onion marinate until the beans are done.

When the beans are ready, remove them from the oven and leave them, covered, to cool for a bit. Then remove and discard the herb sprigs and garlic cloves. (At this point, you can use the beans as a base for soup or other dishes.)

Spoon the beans and a few spoonfuls of their broth into a wide, shallow bowl or deep plate. Drain the onion slices and scatter them over the beans. Sprinkle the parsley on top and drizzle generously with oil to finish. Serve warm.

Crispy Roast Potatoes

The best potatoes I've ever had come from near the city of Avezzano in Abruzzo, where they are cultivated in an ancient lake bed that is said to be full of minerals. They have golden flesh and are rich in earthy flavor and crispy-creamy when roasted. To conjure that flavor and texture with supermarket Yukon golds, I use the parboiling trick: a quick plunge in boiling water before roasting turns them golden brown and crispy on the outside and creamy and tender on the inside.

Fine sea salt

6 medium-large Yukon gold or other yellow potatoes, 2½–3 lb (1.1–1.4 kg), peeled and cut into 3-inch (8-cm) wedges

Extra-virgin olive oil, for drizzling

Freshly ground black pepper

Leaves of 1 fresh rosemary sprig, finely chopped, for garnish (optional)

MAKES 4 SERVINGS

Preheat the oven to 425°F (220°C).

Bring a large pot of water to a boil and salt it generously. Drop in the potatoes, in batches if necessary to avoid crowding, and boil for 3 minutes, no longer. They should remain fairly crisp. Drain well and transfer to a large sheet pan. Drizzle generously with oil, using at least ¼ cup (60 ml), and season with a generous grinding or two of pepper. Use your hands or a spatula to toss the potatoes to coat them well with the oil and pepper. Spread them out on the sheet pan.

Roast the potatoes for 30 minutes. Turn and stir them and continue to roast until golden brown and crispy on the outside and tender inside, 20–30 minutes longer.

Spoon the potatoes onto a platter, garnish with the rosemary, if using, and serve.

DOLCI
SWEETS

A Trio of Amaretti

Made with ground almonds, sugar, and egg white, these tender, tempting, naturally gluten-free cookies can be tossed together in minutes. Once you've got the basic formula down, you can make all sorts of appealing variations, sprinkling in citrus zest or chopped candied peel, adding pistachios along with almonds, or mixing in cocoa powder. Here are three of my favorite flavor combinations; feel free to try your own. The pistachio variation comes from my friend Jessica Botta. I like to garnish half of the cookies with a pistachio and half with a small piece of candied orange peel, but you can garnish as you wish. For the chocolate amaretti, the deep, bitter flavor of cocoa goes beautifully with the taste of buttery, lightly toasted almonds. Use a top-quality unsweetened cocoa powder; I like Vermont-based Lake Champlain brand.

EACH VARIATION MAKES ABOUT 24 AMARETTI

Lemon Amaretti

2 cups (280 g) blanched whole almonds, plus 24 for garnish

1 cup (200 g) granulated sugar

⅛ teaspoon fine sea salt

1 teaspoon finely grated lemon zest

2 large egg whites, at room temperature

¼ teaspoon fresh lemon juice, plus more if needed

¼–½ teaspoon pure almond extract

½ cup (60 g) confectioners' sugar

Preheat the oven to 350°F (180°C). Spread the 2 cups (280 g) almonds on a small sheet pan and toast until they have turned just a shade darker and are fragrant, 7–8 minutes. Pour onto a plate and let cool to room temperature.

Reduce the oven temperature to 325°F (165°C). Line a large sheet pan with parchment paper and stack it on top of a second sheet of the same size. (Stacking the pans will prevent the bottom of the amaretti from browning too quickly or spreading too much. If you only have 1 sheet pan, don't worry. Just be sure to monitor the baking.)

In a food processor, combine the cooled almonds, granulated sugar, and salt and pulse until the nuts are coarsely ground. Add the lemon zest and pulse until the nuts are finely ground. Take care not to overprocess or the mixture will form clumps. Transfer to a bowl and set aside.

In a clean stainless-steel or glass bowl, using an electric mixer, beat the egg whites on medium-low speed until frothy. Add the lemon juice, increase the speed to high, and continue to beat until medium-stiff peaks form (their tips should curl slightly when the beater is lifted).

Fold one-third of the egg whites into the ground nut mixture and add the almond extract, using ¼ teaspoon for a more subtle bitter almond flavor and ½ teaspoon for a more pronounced flavor. Fold in another third of the egg whites, taking care to incorporate them thoroughly. You don't have to be too gentle here. What you're aiming for is a dense, sticky dough that you can form into balls. If the mixture is still dry and crumbly, fold in all the remaining egg white or as much as needed to create a dense, somewhat sticky ball of dough. If the dough is still crumbly after you've added all the egg white, add a teaspoon or so of lemon juice or water. Go easy on the liquid, however. You want the amaretti to hold a nice puffy shape when baked, and if the dough is too slack, the cookies will spread in the oven.

Put the confectioners' sugar into a shallow bowl. Using a small scoop or a 1-tablespoon measure, scoop the dough into small balls. If you want to be meticulous, you can weigh each ball. Each should weigh about ¾ oz (21–22 g) and you should end up with 24 balls. As they are shaped, roll them in the confectioners' sugar and place them on the prepared sheet pan, arranging them in 6 rows of 4 balls each, spaced evenly apart. Gently press an almond into the center of each cookie.

Bake the cookies until they have puffed up and small cracks have formed on top but they are still soft in the center, about 20 minutes. If you are using just 1 pan rather than 2 stacked pans, start checking them after 15 minutes. They should brown only slightly.

Let cool on the pan on a wire rack for 10 minutes. Then, using an offset spatula, transfer the cookies to the rack and let cool completely. They will keep in an airtight container at room temperature for up to 1 week.

Recipe continues

Pistachio Amaretti with Candied Orange Peel and Chamomile

¾ cup (100 g) blanched whole almonds

1¼ cups (150 g) raw pistachios, plus 12 for garnish

1 cup (200 g) granulated sugar

⅛ teaspoon fine sea salt

1 tablespoon chamomile powder (see Cook's Note)

1 tablespoon finely chopped candied orange peel, plus twelve ½-inch (12-mm) pieces candied peel for garnish

2 large egg whites, at room temperature

¼ teaspoon fresh lemon juice

¼ teaspoon pure almond extract

½ cup (60 g) confectioners' sugar

Preheat the oven to 350°F (180°C), then toast the almonds as directed for the Lemon Amaretti (page 152). Reduce the oven temperature to 325°F (165°C).

Continue to follow the directions for Lemon Amaretti with these changes: Pulse the pistachios along with the toasted almonds, granulated sugar, and salt until the nuts are coarsely ground, then pulse in the chamomile powder and candied peel until the nuts are finely ground. Proceed with the recipe as directed, beating the egg whites with the lemon juice, combining the ground nuts, beaten egg whites, and almond extract, forming the dough into balls, and rolling them in the confectioners' sugar. Reserve the 12 pistachios and the 12 candied peel pieces for garnish.

Bake the cookies as directed. As soon as they are removed from the oven, press the pistachios into the center of 12 cookies and the candied peel pieces into the center of the remaining 12 cookies. Let cool and store as directed.

Chocolate Amaretti

2 cups (280 g) blanched whole almonds

1 cup (200 g) granulated sugar

⅛ teaspoon fine sea salt

3 tablespoons unsweetened cocoa powder

2 large egg whites, at room temperature

¼ teaspoon fresh lemon juice

¼–½ teaspoon pure almond extract

½ cup (60 g) confectioners' sugar

Preheat the oven to 350°F (180°C), then toast the almonds as directed for the Lemon Amaretti (page 152). Reduce the oven temperature to 325°F (165°C).

Continue to follow the directions for Lemon Amaretti with these changes: Pulse the toasted almonds, granulated sugar, and salt until the nuts are coarsely ground, then pulse in the cocoa powder until the nuts are finely ground. Proceed with the recipe as directed, beating the egg whites with the lemon juice, combining the ground nuts, beaten egg whites, and almond extract, forming the dough into balls, and rolling them in the confectioners' sugar. No garnish is added before or after baking.

Bake, cool, and store the cookies as directed.

Wine Cookies for Dipping

These rustic cookies are typical of Lazio, the region that includes Rome, and its neighbor, Abruzzo. The ingredients evoke the harvest season: wine and olive oil are the primary components along with flour, sugar, and aniseed. The cookies can be made with white or red wine, but in Abruzzo it is customary to use Montepulciano d'Abruzzo. You can add a pinch of baking powder or baking soda to give them an airier texture, but I prefer them dense and crunchy—just right for dipping into a glass of wine or mug of coffee.

¾ cup (180 ml) Montepulciano d'Abruzzo or other full-bodied wine

¾ cup (180 ml) extra-virgin olive oil

¾ cup (150 g) sugar, plus more for dipping

4 ½ cups (540 g) unbleached all-purpose flour, plus more for dusting

¼ teaspoon fine sea salt

2 teaspoons aniseed

MAKES 40–50 COOKIES

In a stand mixer fitted with the paddle attachment, combine the wine, oil, and sugar and mix on low speed to dissolve the sugar. Add three-fourths of the flour (about 3 ½ cups/435 g), the salt, and the aniseed and mix on low until the flour is absorbed. Add the remaining one-fourth of the flour and mix on low until the dough comes together. It should be dense, somewhat ragged, and shiny.

Turn the dough out onto a lightly floured work surface and knead it briefly. It will be somewhat rough textured. Form it into a ball, cover it with a bowl, and let it rest at room temperature for 30 minutes.

Preheat the oven to 375°F (190°C). Line 2 or 3 large sheet pans with parchment paper.

Fill a small bowl with sugar for dipping. Cut off a golf ball–size piece of dough and roll it into a rope about 4 inches (10 cm) long and slightly thinner than your pinkie. Note that this oil-rich dough tends to break apart as you roll. Simply press it together and reroll. Bring the ends of the rope together and pinch to form a ciambella (ring), or cross one end over the other to make a torcetto (cross). Dip the top of the cookie into the sugar to coat it and place it on a prepared sheet pan. Continue shaping and dipping until all the dough is used up, spacing the cookies about 1 inch (2.5 cm) apart on the pans.

Bake 1 sheet pan at a time until the cookies are browned along the edges, 20–22 minutes. Let cool on the pan on a wire rack for a few minutes, then, using an offset spatula, transfer to the rack and let cool completely before serving. The cookies will keep in an airtight container at room temperature for at least a week unless you eat them sooner (you will).

Iced Coffeehouse Biscotti

One of the lovely things about biscotti is that you can make them as small or as large as you please. These are meant to be the latter, as long as the length of your hand. That makes them just the right size for dunking in coffee, rather than the more genteel dipping in wine, as is customary with bite-size biscotti.

2 cups (250 g) unbleached all-purpose flour, plus more for the work surface

1 cup (200 g) sugar

½ teaspoon baking powder

¼ teaspoon fine sea salt

Finely grated zest of 1 small orange

¾ cup (105 g) skinned hazelnuts, toasted

2 large eggs, lightly beaten, plus 1 egg, lightly beaten, if needed

3 tablespoons hazelnut, sunflower, or olive oil

1 teaspoon pure vanilla extract

3 oz (90 g) bittersweet chocolate, coarsely chopped

3 oz (90 g) milk chocolate, coarsely chopped

MAKES 16 LARGE BISCOTTI

Preheat the oven to 350°F (180°C). Line a large sheet pan with parchment paper.

In a stand mixer fitted with the paddle attachment, combine the flour, sugar, baking powder, salt, orange zest, and hazelnuts and mix on low speed to blend all of the ingredients and break up some of the nuts. Increase the speed to medium, add the 2 beaten eggs, the hazelnut oil, and vanilla, and mix until a soft, slightly sticky dough forms. If the dough seems dry, beat in as much of the remaining egg, adding it in dribbles, as needed to achieve the desired consistency.

Transfer the dough to a lightly floured work surface and pat it into a loaf about 4 inches (10 cm) wide and 12 inches (30 cm) long. Transfer the loaf to the prepared sheet pan and press down to flatten it out a bit and make the top even.

Bake until lightly browned and just set, 30–35 minutes. It should be springy to the touch with cracks on the surface. Let cool on the pan on a wire rack for 5 minutes. Slide an offset spatula under the loaf to loosen it and transfer it to the rack. Let cool for 20 minutes longer. Reduce the oven temperature to 300°F (150°C).

Transfer the cooled loaf to a cutting board. Using a Santoku-style knife or serrated bread knife, cut the loaf crosswise into slices ¾ inch (2 cm) thick. Arrange the slices upright on the sheet and bake until lightly browned, about 15 minutes. Transfer them to the rack and let cool completely. They will become crisp as they cool.

Put the bittersweet chocolate into a heatproof bowl over (not touching) barely simmering water in a saucepan. Heat, stirring gently now and again, until the chocolate is melted and smooth. To melt in a microwave, put the chocolate into a microwave-safe bowl and microwave at 50 percent power in 30-second intervals, stirring after each interval, until melted and smooth. Melt the milk chocolate the same way.

Arrange the cooled slices upright on the rack and set the rack over the sheet pan still lined with parchment. Dip a fork into the melted bittersweet chocolate and wave it back and forth over the biscotti to create thin and fat drizzles. Repeat with the melted milk chocolate. Place the sheet pan in a cool spot for 30 minutes to set the chocolate. The biscotti will keep in an airtight container at room temperature for up to 10 days.

Pineapple-Coconut Sorbetto

The Italian word for pineapple is ananas (AH-nah-nas). It's one of the funniest words in the Italian language (go ahead and say it), probably because it's not Italian at all. The word, like the fruit, has its origins in South America. Pineapple arrived in Italy a few centuries ago by way of Spanish and English explorers. It is very popular; every gelateria serves a pineapple gelato or sorbetto. Coconut milk gives this version a fresh tropical twist.

2 lb (1 kg) fresh pineapple chunks (about 6 cups)

1¾ cups (350 g) vanilla sugar (see Cook's Note)

3⅓ cups (780 ml) water

3 lemon zest strips (no white pith)

1 cup (30 g) firmly packed fresh mint leaves, coarsely chopped

⅔ cup (160 ml) whole milk

⅔ cup (160 ml) coconut milk

MAKES 1 QT (1 L)

COOK'S NOTE
You can purchase vanilla sugar, but it is very easy to make at home if you plan ahead. Simply bury a vanilla bean in your sugar canister and let sit for 1–2 weeks to infuse the sugar.

In a blender, working in batches, purée the pineapple until smooth. Set aside.

In a large, heavy-bottomed saucepan, stir together the vanilla sugar and water, then drop in the lemon zest. Set over medium-low heat and cook, stirring gently, until the sugar is completely dissolved. Raise the heat to medium and bring the sugar syrup to a boil. Reduce the heat to medium-low and simmer until thickened to a light syrup, about 10 minutes.

Remove the syrup from the heat and stir in the pineapple purée and mint. Cover the pan and let the mixture steep at room temperature for 3–4 hours. Strain the mixture through a fine-mesh sieve into a bowl and stir in the whole milk and coconut milk. Transfer to an airtight container and refrigerate until well chilled, at least 4 hours or up to overnight.

Transfer the pineapple mixture to an ice cream machine and churn according to the manufacturer's instructions until thickened and frozen. Transfer to an airtight container and freeze until ready to serve.

If you don't have an ice cream machine, pour the pineapple mixture into a sturdy container with a tight-fitting lid and freeze for 2–3 hours. Purée the mixture with an immersion blender and return it to the freezer for another 2–3 hours. Repeat the blending step two more times to break up the sorbetto and then one more time 30 minutes before serving.

Lemon Semifreddo

A slice of this frozen lemon dessert is my favorite way to end a summer dinner party. The combination of bright lemon, whipped mascarpone cream, and crunchy amaretti offers just the right balance of tart, sweet, cool, and creamy. Slice it thickly and garnish each serving with fresh berries for a splash of color.

6 large egg yolks

1 cup (200 g) sugar

Pinch of fine sea salt

½ cup (120 ml) fresh lemon juice (from about 3 lemons)

2 tablespoons finely grated lemon zest

1 tablespoon limoncello

Sunflower or other neutral oil, for the pan

1½ cups (350 ml) cold heavy cream (see Cook's Note, page 160)

½ cup (115 g) cold mascarpone

10–12 small, crunchy amaretti cookies

Berries, such as blueberries, blackberries, or strawberries, for serving

MAKES 8–10 SERVINGS

Set a fine-mesh sieve over a medium bowl. Fill a second, slightly larger bowl with ice and rest the medium bowl with the sieve in the ice. Set aside. Fill a medium saucepan halfway with water and set over medium-high heat. Bring to a boil over high heat, then reduce the heat to maintain a gentle simmer.

To make a lemon curd, in a medium heatproof bowl, whisk together the egg yolks, sugar, and salt until blended. Whisk in the lemon juice and zest. Set the bowl over the saucepan, making sure the bottom of the bowl is not touching the water. Cook, whisking constantly, until the egg mixture has thickened to an almost spoonable consistency, 7–8 minutes.

As soon as the curd is thick enough, remove it from the heat and stir in the limoncello. Pass it through the sieve into the bowl on ice and stir for 1–2 minutes. Remove the bowl from the ice, cover with plastic wrap, pressing the wrap directly onto the curd, and refrigerate until thoroughly chilled, about 2 hours.

Lightly coat the bottom and sides of an 8 ½ x 4 ½-inch (21.5 x 11.5-cm) loaf pan with oil. Line the pan with plastic wrap, letting some excess hang over the ends and sides.

In a bowl, using an electric mixer on medium-high speed or a whisk, whip together the cream and mascarpone just until stiff peaks form. Gently fold in the lemon curd just until incorporated. Pour half of the lemon cream into the prepared loaf pan and smooth the surface. Arrange the amaretti on top, two by two, along the length of the pan. Cover with the remaining lemon cream and smooth the surface. Cover the pan with plastic wrap and freeze. (The semifreddo will keep in the freezer for up to 1 week.)

To serve, unmold the semifreddo onto a cutting board, lifting off the pan and peeling off the wrap. Let stand for 5 minutes to soften. Trim off the ends, then slice the loaf. Serve with berries scattered on top.

Fig and Wine Gelato

Red wine and figs belong together. Wine enhances the fruit's own notes of honey and berry while adding depth and a splash of sophistication. It makes for pretty ice cream, too, the wine-plumped figs adding a rose blush. This is a no-churn ice cream, as easy to make as mashing up some fruit and whipping some cream. Any fig variety will do here, though the darker-skinned ones will give you those gorgeous ruby flecks. I use Brown Turkey figs from my trusty little tree.

1 lb (450 g) ripe figs, such as Brown Turkey, stemmed and quartered lengthwise, plus figs, stemmed and halved lengthwise, for garnish

¼–⅓ cup (50–65 g) granulated sugar

1 tablespoon fresh lemon juice

⅔ cup (160 ml) dry red wine

¼ teaspoon ground cinnamon

1 can (14 oz/400 g) sweetened condensed milk

2 cups (475 ml) cold heavy cream (see Cook's Note)

2 tablespoons confectioners' sugar

1 teaspoon pure vanilla extract

MAKES 1 QT (1 L)

COOK'S NOTE
When whipping cream, it's best to start off with everything cold. Chill the bowl and the whisk or beaters in the freezer for about 30 minutes and make sure the cream is straight out of the refrigerator.

Place a metal 9 x 5-inch (23 x 13-cm) loaf pan in the freezer to chill.

In a heavy-bottomed saucepan, combine the figs, granulated sugar (amount depends on the sweetness of the figs), and lemon juice and stir to dissolve the sugar. Set the saucepan over medium-low heat and use a potato masher to mash up the fruit a bit as it starts to heat up. Bring to a gentle simmer and cook, stirring often, just until the figs have softened slightly, about 5 minutes. Raise the heat to medium and pour in the wine. Simmer until most of the wine has been absorbed and what's left has thickened to a light syrupy consistency, about 10 minutes. Reduce the heat if necessary to prevent scorching.

Transfer the mixture to a large bowl and stir in the cinnamon. Let cool to room temperature, about 30 minutes, then whisk in the condensed milk.

In a bowl, whip the cream by hand with a whisk or with a handheld mixer on medium-high speed until it begins to thicken. Add the confectioners' sugar and vanilla and whip until stiff peaks form. Gently fold the whipped cream into the fig mixture just until fully incorporated.

Scrape the mixture into the chilled loaf pan and smooth the top with a spatula. Cover tightly with plastic wrap (I secure the wrap onto the pan with a rubber band). Freeze until solid, at least 4 hours.

To serve, remove the gelato from the freezer 5–10 minutes before serving to allow it to soften a bit before scooping. Scoop into bowls and garnish each serving with a fig half or two. (This gelato is also delicious drizzled with bittersweet chocolate sauce.)

Peach Frangipane Crostata

At its most basic, a crostata is a rustic lattice-topped, jam-filled tart composed of buttery pastry called pasta frolla. But that is just the beginning. A crostata can be as simple or as sumptuous as you like. You can fill it with pastry cream or chopped nuts, chocolate-studded ricotta, or lemon mousse. The variations are pretty much countless. This summer recipe combines ripe peaches with a layer of frangipane, a rich almond cream that pairs beautifully with the stone fruit.

PASTA FROLLA

2 cups (250 g) unbleached all-purpose flour, plus more for dusting

⅔ cup (75 g) confectioners' sugar

¼ teaspoon fine sea salt

Finely grated zest of 1 lemon (about 1 tablespoon)

½ cup plus 3 tablespoons (160 g) cold unsalted butter, cut into ½-inch (12-mm) cubes

1 large egg

1 large egg yolk

PRESERVES

1½ lb (680 g) ripe peaches, halved, pitted, peeled, and cut into slices ½ inch (12 mm) thick, or 1 lb (450 g) frozen sliced peaches

1 cup (210 g) firmly packed light brown sugar

1 tablespoon fresh lemon juice

¼ teaspoon ground cinnamon

Pinch of freshly grated nutmeg

To make the pasta frolla, in a food processor, combine the all-purpose flour, confectioners' sugar, salt, and lemon zest and pulse briefly to mix. Distribute the butter around the bowl and pulse until the mixture is crumbly. Add the egg and egg yolk and process until the dough begins to clump together.

Turn the dough out onto a lightly floured work surface and gather it together into a ball. Form the dough into 2 disks, one slightly larger than the other. Wrap each disk tightly in plastic wrap and refrigerate until well chilled, at least 1 hour (overnight is fine). Remove the dough from the refrigerator 30 minutes before rolling it out.

To make the preserves, in a heavy-bottomed saucepan over low heat, combine the peaches, brown sugar, and lemon juice and cook, stirring often, until the sugar is dissolved, about 5 minutes. Raise the heat to medium-high and bring to a boil. Adjust the heat to maintain a lively simmer and cook, stirring often, until the peach slices are tender but still intact and the mixture has thickened to a syrupy consistency, about 10 minutes. Stir in the cinnamon and nutmeg and simmer for about 5 minutes longer. The preserves are ready if, when you drag a heat-resistant spatula or wooden spoon across the bottom of the pan, it leaves a path that does not fill immediately.

Scrape the mixture into a heatproof bowl and let cool completely. (At this point, the preserves can be refrigerated until ready to use.)

To make the frangipane, in the food processor, combine the almond flour, granulated sugar, butter, egg, almond and vanilla extracts, and salt and pulse until the mixture forms a spreadable paste. Scrape into a bowl.

FRANGIPANE

¾ cup (85 g) almond flour or almond meal

⅓ cup (65 g) granulated sugar

6 tablespoons (90 g) unsalted butter, at cool room temperature, cut into pieces

1 large egg

¼ teaspoon pure almond extract

¼ teaspoon pure vanilla extract

⅛ teaspoon fine sea salt

Confectioners' sugar and/ or vanilla gelato, for serving (optional)

MAKES 8 SERVINGS

When you are ready to assemble the crostata, remove the pasta frolla from the refrigerator. Place a sheet pan on the middle rack of the oven and preheat the oven to 350°F (180°C). Have ready a 9-inch (23-cm) fluted tart pan with a removable bottom.

Lightly dust a work surface and a rolling pin with flour. Place the larger disk of pasta frolla on the floured surface and roll out into a 12-inch (30-cm) round about ¼ inch (6 mm) thick, lifting and turning the dough as you roll to prevent sticking and to create an even round. Gently wrap the dough around the rolling pin, unroll it over the tart pan, and gently press it into the pan without stretching it. Use the palm of your hand or the rolling pin to trim off the excess. Refrigerate the crostata base while you roll out the second piece of dough.

Roll out the smaller piece into a 10-inch (25-cm) round the same way. Use a fluted pastry wheel to cut it into strips as narrow or as wide as you like. Remove the crostata base from the refrigerator and spread the frangipane over the bottom in an even layer. Using a slotted spoon, spoon the cooled peaches over the frangipane in an even layer, letting the excess syrup drip back into the bowl (you can discard the syrup or save it to drizzle on top at serving time). Position the strips of pastry on top of the peaches in a crisscross lattice pattern. You can weave the strips if you like, but the dough is fragile and tends to tear, so it's not necessary (nor is it traditional). Press the ends of the strips into the edge of the tart shell to secure them and trim off the excess.

Set the crostata on the heated sheet pan and bake until the crust is golden brown and the interior is bubbling, about 40 minutes. Remove the sheet pan from the oven and transfer the tart pan to a wire rack to cool until it can be handled, about 30 minutes.

Carefully slip off the pan ring, then use a large offset spatula to transfer the crostata from the metal tart base to a serving plate. Serve warm or at room temperture. Dust with confectioners' sugar, if you like, just before serving. For an extra-lavish touch, top each serving with a scoop of vanilla gelato and drizzle with some of the leftover caramelized peach syrup.

Kiwi Fruit Salad with Mascarpone Cream

Did you know that Italy is one of the world's largest producers of kiwifruits? The first time I saw them growing was in a citrus grove in Liguria a few years ago. The plants were arranged in rows; the leaves and vines formed a beautiful pergola from which the fruits hung like ornaments. Beneath the kiwi's fuzzy brown skin is lime-green flesh that, when ripe, is juicy and zesty, with an appealing crunch from tiny black seeds. Mixed with fresh blueberries, tangy-sweet pineapple, and tart pomegranate, it makes a refreshing fruit salad.

FRUIT SALAD

6 ripe kiwifruits

1 cup (140 g) blueberries

1 cup (155 g) fresh
pineapple chunks

½ cup (70 g) pomegranate
arils (seeds)

2 tablespoons honey

2 tablespoons fresh lime juice

MASCARPONE CREAM

½ cup (120 ml) cold heavy cream
(see Cook's Note, page 160)

2 tablespoons cold mascarpone

1 tablespoon confectioners' sugar

MAKES 6 SERVINGS

To make the fruit salad, peel the kiwis and cut them into quarters. Cut the quarters into bite-size pieces and put them into a bowl. Fold in the blueberries, pineapple chunks, and pomegranate arils.

In a small bowl, whisk together the honey and lime juice to make a dressing. Pour the dressing over the fruit and toss gently.

To make the mascarpone cream, in a bowl, using an electric mixer on medium speed or a whisk, whip together the cream and mascarpone just until the mixture begins to thicken. Add the confectioners' sugar and continue to whip on medium-high speed until stiff peaks form.

Spoon the fruit salad into individual bowls. Top each bowl with a dollop of mascarpone cream and serve.

Chocolate Almond Torte

Torta caprese, as this rich cake is called in Italian, originated on the island of Capri. There are many variations, some with more nuts than chocolate, some more dense than airy, some with liqueur, and some that add a pinch of baking powder to assist leavening. My version is a true torte because it contains no artificial leavening. It relies on almond flour, chocolate, and butter for richness, and air beaten separately into the egg yolks and whites for lightness.

½ cup (115 g) unsalted butter, cut into pieces, plus more for the pan

Unbleached all-purpose flour, for the pan

1 cup (140 g) blanched whole almonds

8 oz (225 g) bittersweet chocolate, chopped

1 cup (200 g) granulated sugar

4 large eggs, separated

2 tablespoons brewed espresso, liqueur such as Kahlúa (coffee liqueur) or Amaretto, brandy, or grappa

½ teaspoon pure vanilla extract

¼ teaspoon fine sea salt

Confectioners' sugar, for dusting

Whipped cream, for serving

MAKES 8–10 SERVINGS

Preheat the oven to 350°F (180°C). Butter the bottom and sides of a 9-inch (23-cm) round springform pan, then dust with flour, tapping out the excess.

Spread the almonds on a small sheet pan or a pie pan and toast until they have turned just a shade darker and are fragrant, 7–8 minutes. Pour onto a plate and let cool to room temperature, then transfer to a food processor and pulse until finely ground. Don't overprocess the nuts or they will release their oil, causing clumps. Set aside.

Put the butter and chocolate into a heatproof bowl over (not touching) barely simmering water in a saucepan. Heat, stirring gently now and again to mix, until the butter and chocolate are melted and smooth. Remove from the heat as soon as they have melted and let the mixture cool briefly.

In a large bowl, whisk together the egg yolks and ¾ cup (150 g) of the granulated sugar until light and creamy (or use a handheld mixer on medium speed). Add the espresso, vanilla, and salt and beat until blended. Gradually whisk in the cooled chocolate-butter mixture until well mixed, then fold in the ground almonds just until evenly distributed.

In a bowl, using an electric mixer, beat the egg whites on medium-low speed until foamy. With the mixer on medium speed, slowly pour in the remaining ¼ cup (50 g) granulated sugar and whip until the whites are glossy and hold firm peaks when the beaters are lifted.

With a rubber spatula, fold one-third of the whites into the chocolate mixture to lighten it. Then, using a scooping and folding motion, gently incorporate the remaining whites just until no white streaks remain. Pour the batter into the prepared pan.

Bake the torte until just set and the top is firm with some cracks, 30–35 minutes. A cake tester or toothpick inserted into the center should come out nearly clean, with just a few cake crumbs or tiny bits of batter on it.

Let cool in the pan on a wire rack for 5 minutes; it will deflate a bit and the cracks will become more prominent. Run a narrow offset spatula or a thin knife around the inside edge of the pan to loosen the torte sides, then unclasp and carefully remove the pan ring. Let the cake cool completely before serving. This torte is delicate, so I don't recommend inverting it to remove the springform pan base. (But if you are an intrepid baker, go for it.) You can use a large offfset spatula to remove it from the pan base and transer it to a decorative platter. Or, if it seems too fragile, transfer it, still on the base, to the platter. Dust with confectioners' sugar.

Slice into wedges and top each serving with a dollop of whipped cream.

Pistachio Cake with Pistachio-Ricotta Cream

This is a simple cake masquerading as a fancy cake. The cake itself is a pistachio sponge—light and airy and with a gentle flavor. The ricotta filling, tinged pale green with pistachio cream, is both luxurious and ridiculously easy to make. You don't have to worry about frosting here. A shower of confectioners' sugar and a ring of chopped pistachios around the top are all this cake needs.

PISTACHIO CAKE

Unsalted butter, for the pan

6 large eggs, separated, at room temperature

¼ teaspoon fresh lemon juice

Pinch of fine sea salt

¾ cup (150 g) granulated sugar

Finely grated zest of 1 lemon

2 tablespoons pistachio cream (see Cook's Note), optional

2 cups (220 g) pistachio flour (see Cook's Note) or finely ground raw pistachios

PISTACHIO-RICOTTA CREAM

2 cups (450 g) whole-milk ricotta cheese, well-drained (see Cook's Note, page 79)

⅔ cup (160 ml) heavy cream

⅓ cup (40 g) confectioners' sugar

2–4 tablespoons (40–80 g) pistachio cream (optional)

½ teaspoon vanilla paste or pure vanilla extract

FOR GARNISH

Confectioners' sugar, for dusting

¼ cup (30 g) chopped pistachios

MAKES 10–12 SERVINGS

To make the cake, preheat the oven to 325°F (165°C). Butter the bottom and sides of a 9-inch (23-cm) round springform pan with at least 2 ¾-inch (7-cm) sides. Line the bottom with a round of parchment paper and butter the parchment.

In a stand mixer fitted with the whip attachment, beat the egg whites on low speed until foamy. Add the lemon juice and salt, increase the speed to medium, and beat until the whites hold soft peaks. Increase the speed to medium-high and add 6 tablespoons (75 g) of the granulated sugar, 1 tablespoon at a time. When all the sugar is incorporated, increase the mixer speed to high and beat the whites until they are glossy and hold medium-firm peaks that curve slightly at the tips. Set aside.

In a clean mixer bowl, beat the egg yolks with the remaining 6 tablespoons (75 g) granulated sugar at medium speed until thick, pale, and ribbony, about 4 minutes. Add the lemon zest and the pistachio cream, if using, and beat until well mixed.

Using a rubber spatula, gently fold one-third of the egg whites into the yolk mixture to lighten it. Then, using a scooping and folding motion, gently incorporate the remaining whites. Gently fold in half of the pistachio flour, taking care not to deflate the batter, then gently fold in the remaining flour. Scrape the batter into the prepared pan, smoothing the surface.

Bake the cake until it is golden on top and a cake tester inserted near the center comes out clean, about 40 minutes.

Recipe continues

Pistachio Cake continued

Pistachio flour is not as widely available as almond flour, but it is available online (giannettiartisans.com) and, while expensive, worth seeking out for its emerald color and consistent texture. If using raw pistachios, look for ones that are peeled as well as shelled so they are mostly bright green. Pulse them in a food processor until finely ground. Don't overprocess the nuts or they will release their oils, causing clumping.

Like pistachio flour, pistachio cream is a small luxury but also worth the occasional splurge. It has the consistency of Nutella and tastes of pure pistachio (and sugar). You can find it online at gustiamo.com and olio2go.com.

Let the cake cool in the pan on a wire rack for 20 minutes. Run a narrow offset spatula or a thin knife around the inside edge of the pan to loosen the cake sides, then unclasp and carefully remove the pan ring and let cool for 30 minutes longer. Gently invert the cake onto a plate, lift off the pan bottom, and peel off the parchment. Turn the cake right side up on the rack and let cool to room temperature.

To make the pistachio-ricotta cream, pass the drained ricotta through a fine-mesh sieve set over a bowl. This step is tedious but necessary to get a smooth, creamy filling.

Transfer the ricotta to a clean mixer bowl and add the cream. Fit the mixer with the clean whip attachment and beat on low speed until well mixed, then increase the speed to medium-high. When the mixture starts to thicken, add the confectioners' sugar, pistachio cream (if using), and vanilla, increase the speed to high, and beat until thickened and smooth.

To assemble the cake, invert the cake once more so it is bottom side up. Using a long, serrated knife, slice the cake horizontally into 2 layers. Set aside the flat top layer. Place the other layer, cut side up, on a serving plate and spread the pistachio-ricotta cream thickly and evenly over it. Set the other layer, cut side down, on top. To finish, dust the top with confectioners' sugar and sprinkle the pistachios around the top edge of the cake.

Sambuca Apple Cake

Chopped apples get a nice soak in a sambuca bath before being folded into the batter. The result is a fragrant, tender cake with a subtle anise kick. Use a mix of sweet and tart apples to give the cake a more complex flavor. I first enjoyed this cake at the Marchese del Grillo bed-and-breakfast in Sulmona, a medieval city ringed with mountains in the heart of Abruzzo. Owner Marta Carrozza was kind enough to share the recipe.

1 cup (240 ml) sunflower or other neutral oil

4 apples (1½ lb/680 g total weight), preferably a mix of sweet and tart

⅓ cup (80 ml) sambuca or other anise-flavored liqueur

4 large eggs

1½ cups (300 g) granulated sugar

Finely grated zest of 1 lemon

½ teaspoon pure vanilla extract

2½ cups (315 g) unbleached all-purpose flour

½ teaspoon fine sea salt

2 teaspoons baking powder

Confectioners' sugar, for dusting

MAKES 8 SERVINGS

Preheat the oven to 350°F (180°C). Oil the bottom and sides of a 9-inch (23-cm) round springform pan with a scant 1 tablespoon of the oil. Line the bottom with a round of parchment paper and use the rest of the spoonful of oil to lightly oil the parchment.

Peel and core the apples and cut them into bite-size pieces. As you work, put them into a bowl and toss gently with the sambuca to prevent browning. Once all the apples are cut, toss gently to make sure they are thoroughly coated, then let sit while you mix the other ingredients.

In a large bowl, whisk together the eggs and granulated sugar until light. Whisk in the lemon zest, the remaining oil, and the vanilla until thoroughly incorporated. In a medium bowl, stir together the flour, salt, and baking powder. Stir the flour mixture into the egg mixture, mixing well. Fold in the apples and sambuca, distributing the apples evenly. Pour the batter into the prepared pan.

Bake the cake until the top is golden brown and a cake tester inserted into the center comes out clean, 1–1¼ hours. If the top is browned before the cake is done, gently lay a piece of aluminum foil over the top and finish baking.

Let the cake cool in the pan on a wire rack for 20–30 minutes. Run a narrow offset spatula or a thin knife around the inside edge of the pan to loosen the cake sides, then unclasp and gently remove the pan ring. Let the cake cool to room temperature.

Invert the cake onto a plate, lift off the pan bottom, and peel off the parchment. Turn the cake upright on a serving plate. Dust with confectioners' sugar just before serving.

Lemon-Rosemary Cornmeal Cake with Lemon Syrup

A slice of simple lemon cake can be breakfast or dessert. Either way, the burst of citrus and rosemary will lift your mood. Be sure to use fine-grind cornmeal, as coarse-grind will make the cake gritty (not very mood lifting!).

CORNMEAL CAKE

½ cup (120 ml) extra-virgin olive oil, plus more for the pan

1 cup (200 g) sugar

2 large eggs, at room temperature

Finely grated zest of 1 lemon

1 tablespoon finely minced fresh rosemary

½ cup (115 g) plain whole-milk Greek yogurt

1 cup plus 2 tablespoons (145 g) unbleached all-purpose flour

½ cup (70 g) fine-grind cornmeal

2 teaspoons baking powder

¼ teaspoon fine sea salt

LEMON SYRUP

¼ cup (60 ml) fresh lemon juice

½ cup (100 g) sugar

Whipped cream, for serving

MAKES 6 SERVINGS

To make the cake, preheat the oven to 350°F (180°C). Lightly coat the bottom and sides of an 8-inch (20-cm) round cake pan with oil. Line the bottom with a round of parchment paper, then lightly coat the parchment with oil.

In a large bowl, whisk together the oil, sugar, eggs, lemon zest, rosemary, and yogurt until well blended. In a separate bowl, whisk together the flour, cornmeal, baking powder, and salt. Pour the flour mixture into the egg mixture, whisking all the while to avoid lumps. Scrape the batter into the prepared pan.

Bake the cake until a cake tester inserted into the center comes out clean, 20–30 minutes. Let cool in the pan on a wire rack for 20–30 minutes. Invert the cake onto a clean surface, lift off the pan, and peel off the parchment. Turn the cake right side up on the rack and set on a sheet pan to catch any drips of syrup.

To make the syrup, in a small, heavy-bottomed saucepan over medium-low heat, combine the lemon juice and sugar and heat, stirring, until the sugar is dissolved. Raise the heat to medium-high and bring to a boil. Boil until thickened to a syrup, 3–4 minutes. Remove from the heat.

Use a pastry brush to brush the surface of the warm cake with the syrup. I like to glaze the cake generously to create a thick, shiny surface. Let the cake cool to room temperature.

Transfer the cake to a decorative plate, slice, and serve. Accompany each serving with a dollop of whipped cream.

Dark Chocolate Panna Cotta
with Amarena Cherries

There's something inherently elegant about finishing a meal with a spoon dessert, even when it's as easy to make as this chocolate panna cotta. Bittersweet chocolate gives the cream a dense, silky texture, and the Cognac adds a touch of luxury. This is a rich dessert, so keep portions small.

3 cups (700 ml) heavy cream

⅓ cup (65 g) superfine sugar

Pinch of fine sea salt

½ vanilla bean

2 ½ teaspoons (1 package) unflavored gelatin

6 oz (170 g) bittersweet chocolate, preferably 72% cacao, chopped

2 tablespoons Cognac

Sunflower or other neutral oil, for the mold

Whipped cream, for serving

6–8 Amarena cherries in syrup, for serving (see Cook's Note)

MAKES 6–8 SERVINGS

COOK'S NOTE
Grown in many parts of Italy, sweet-tart dark Amarena cherries are typically preserved in syrup and used as a garnish in classic desserts from cannoli to zeppole. They are sold in decorative jars and can be purchased online or at specialty markets.

In a deep saucepan, combine 2 ½ cups (580 ml) of the cream, the sugar, and the salt. Split the vanilla bean lengthwise and, using the tip of the knife, scrape the seeds from the pod into the pan. Whisk to incorporate everything and set over medium heat. Bring almost to a boil, then remove from the heat as soon as the cream starts to bubble.

In a small bowl, sprinkle the gelatin over the remaining ½ cup (120 ml) cream and let it bloom for about 10 minutes. Set the bowl over a small saucepan of hot water and whisk until the gelatin dissolves into the cream. It will thicken at first, but keep whisking until it loosens and melts. Whisk the gelatin mixture into the saucepan with the hot cream mixture.

Put the chocolate into a heatproof bowl and slowly add the hot cream mixture, stirring all the while until the chocolate is completely melted. Whisk in the Cognac.

Brush a 5-cup (1.2-l) pudding mold or soufflé dish with oil. Pour in the chocolate cream and let cool to room temperature. Cover tightly and refrigerate until well chilled, at least 4 hours (overnight is fine).

To serve, dip the bottom of the mold in hot water for about 10 seconds. Invert a serving plate over the top of the mold, then flip the mold and plate together to dislodge the panna cotta onto the plate. Spoon into dessert cups or cut into slices and arrange on individual plates. Garnish each serving with a dollop of whipped cream and a cherry.

Coffee Crème Caramel

I've loved this dessert of dark, slightly bitter caramel and rich, slightly bitter espresso since I was a child. But the thought of making it struck fear in my heart. First, there's the making of the caramel, which, if not done correctly, risks seizing up into a crystallized mess. Then there's the baking of the custard in a water bath. If the temperature is too low, the custard won't set properly, and if it is too high, you end up with bubbles that mar what should be a perfectly smooth surface. I'm happy to say that I've mastered this longtime favorite, and you can too. Follow the instructions closely, use the proper equipment—a heavy-bottomed saucepan for the caramel is crucial—and pay attention to visual cues. And remember, even if you have some hiccups the first time around, the process will become easier each time you do it.

CARAMEL

1 cup (200 g) sugar

¼ cup (60 ml) water

COFFEE CRÈME

1 can (14 oz/400 g) sweetened condensed milk

1 cup (240 ml) heavy cream

1 cup (240 ml) whole milk

½ cup (120 ml) brewed espresso

4 large eggs

2 large egg yolks

1 cup (200 g) sugar

MAKES 8 SERVINGS

Preheat the oven to 325°F (165°C).

To make the caramel, have ready a round, ovenproof baking dish. (I use a 2-qt/2-l) ceramic soufflé dish.) Pour the sugar into a heavy-bottomed saucepan and stir in the water. Place over medium-low heat and stir to dissolve the sugar. When the sugar is mostly dissolved, raise the heat to medium and bring to a simmer. The mixture will start to boil, which is what you want. Grasp the pan handle and swirl the mixture around a bit. Do not stir it with a spoon or heat-resistant spatula. Continue to cook, giving it the occasional swirl, until the mixture starts to change color. It will go from clear to opaque and eventually take on a golden tinge. Once that happens, your caramel will form quickly, so watch closely, swirling gently to distribute the heat. When the caramel has turned deep amber and has a rich caramel aroma, remove it from the heat and immediately pour it into the waiting baking dish. Rotate the dish to coat the bottom completely and a little up the sides. Set aside to cool (it will harden quickly).

Fill a kettle with water and bring the water to a boil over high heat. Remove from the heat and let the water cool down a bit.

While the water is heating, make the coffee crème. In a large bowl, whisk together the condensed milk, cream, whole milk, and espresso. Whisk in the eggs, egg yolks, and sugar, mixing well. Pour the mixture through a fine-mesh sieve into the caramel-lined baking dish.

Open the oven door and pull out the rack. Place a large baking pan on the rack. (I use a 12-inch/30-cm round aluminum pan with 2-inch/5-cm sides.) Place the baking dish in the center of the baking pan and carefully pour the hot water into the pan to come halfway up the sides of the baking dish. Carefully slide the rack back into the oven.

Bake the custard until it is nearly set, 60–70 minutes. It should still be jiggly in the center when the dish is gently shaken. Check the custard from time to time as it bakes; if you see that the water in the pan is beginning to simmer or that bubbles are forming around the edges of the custard, reduce the oven temperature to 300°F (150°C).

When the custard is done, remove the pan from the oven. Transfer the baking dish from the water bath to a wire rack and let the custard cool to room temperature. Cover tightly and refrigerate overnight.

To serve, slide a thin paring knife around the inside edge of the baking dish to loosen the custard sides. Invert a serving plate over the baking dish, then flip the mold and plate together to dislodge the custard onto the plate. As you lift off the mold, the caramel will drip over the top and down the sides of the custard. Spoon onto small plates and serve.

MY EVERYDAY ITALIAN PANTRY

A well-stocked pantry has saved me more times than I can count when I was working late and had to scramble to put dinner on the table. I depend on ingredients like good olive oil, bottled tomato passata, anchovies, beans, cheeses, pickled vegetables, nuts, and spices to make a quick sauce or pesto, to add flavor to soups, and to serve as a simple side dish or snack. Here is a list of ingredients you'll find in my pantry and in the recipes in this book.

BEANS AND LEGUMES

Look for imported dried beans in Italian markets and check their harvest date. Old beans remain grainy even after long cooking, so avoid those that are undated and toss those that have been hanging around your pantry for a few years (as I have to do from time to time). Good-quality canned beans are a convenient alternative.

Borlotti: Similar to cranberry beans, borlotti have a mottled pink-and-beige appearance that turns brownish when cooked. They are a common ingredient in *pasta e fagioli*, a classic southern Italian dish, and in minestrone.

Cannellini: Ivory colored, with a fluffy texture when cooked, cannellini are often served warm, drizzled with excellent olive oil and accented with herbs, as a side dish.

Chickpeas: I find the earthy flavor and meaty, slightly crumbly texture of chickpeas even more appealing than the taste and "bite" of beans, so I always keep plenty of canned and dried chickpeas on hand.

CHEESE

Good cheese, like good oil, is essential to the everyday Italian table, whether it's being served as an antipasto, sprinkled on pasta, or stirred into risotto. Because it is so perishable, I tend to buy cheese on an as-needed basis. That said, I always have wedges of **Parmigiano Reggiano** and **pecorino romano** in my refrigerator because I use them so often. They are without a doubt Italy's best-known and most-loved grating cheeses. Here are some other cheeses I use often.

Fontina Valle d'Aosta: A dense, good melting cheese made in the Italian Alps, fontina has a pungent aroma but an appealing nutty, slightly mushroomy flavor.

Gorgonzola: A blue-veined cow's milk cheese produced in Lombardy and Piedmont, Gorgonzola is sold in two styles: Gorgonzola dolce is creamy and soft, while Gorgonzola piccante is aged longer and has a sharper flavor and more crumbly texture.

Mascarpone: A rich, sweet spreadable cow's milk cheese to which cream has been added, mascarpone is dense and buttery. Its texture can vary, however, from soft, like sour cream, to stiff, like frosting.

Mozzarella: The name refers to numerous fresh or briefly aged Italian cheeses that are shaped by pulling and then shaping the curd. The cheese can be made from the milk of cows or water buffalo. Fresh mozzarella, usually packed in brine or whey, is tender and has a rich, milky, tangy flavor.

Scamorza, a slightly aged mozzarella available both plain and smoked, is widely available in Italy but less so in the United States. Burrata, from Puglia, has become almost as popular as mozzarella. It is made from mixing mozzarella curds with cream and enclosing them in a mozzarella pouch. The curds and cream, sans pouch, are known as stracciatella for their raglike appearance.

Ricotta: Literally translating to "recooked," ricotta is a by-product cheese made from the whey left over from cheese making. Most ricotta sold in the United States is cow's milk ricotta, made from whole or skim milk rather than whey. Fresh ricotta has small curds and is spoonable. Ricotta salata is salted ricotta that has been drained and aged slightly. It has a smooth, chalky paste and is good for crumbling. Juniper-smoked ricotta, a delicate, lightly smoked cheese from Abruzzo, is not widely available in the United States, but you can find it online at marcelliformaggi.com.

Sottocenere al tartufo: This semisoft cow's milk cheese from the Veneto region has a thin, ash-coated rind and a smooth paste flecked with black truffle.

Stracciatella: This a fresh, milky cheese made from "shreds" of fresh mozzarella mixed with cream. It's what you find when you slice into a ball of burrata. You can sometimes find containers of stracciatella at well-stocked cheese markets. If it's not available, buy burrata (one or two balls, depending on their size) and slice it open. Scoop out the stracciatella and spoon it onto the crostini. If you like, you can also chop the burrata "skin" in which the stracciatella is enclosed and mix the two together before spooning the mixture onto the crostini. That way, nothing is wasted.

Taleggio: A semisoft washed-rind cow's milk cheese from Lombardy, Taleggio has a strong aroma and a buttery, meaty flavor.

CURED MEATS

Italy has a rich variety of cured meats (*salumi*) from every region. Here is a selection you'll see in recipes in this book.

Guanciale: Salt-cured pork jowl seasoned with garlic, pepper, and woodsy herbs, this fatty cured meat is an essential ingredient particularly in Roman cuisine, where it is used in such iconic dishes as *spaghetti alla carbonara*.

Mortadella: A specialty of Bologna, this oversized sausage is studded with pieces of lard and, often, pistachios, and has a silky-smooth texture.

Pancetta: Pork belly cured with salt, pepper, and spices, pancetta is slightly less fatty than guanciale. It is used in similar preparations, as a flavor base for soups and sauces and to dress pasta.

Prosciutto: Made from pork leg, imported prosciutto di Parma (Parma ham) is cured with salt, air-dried, and aged for more than a year. The best prosciutto has just the right balance of salty meat and silky, sweet fat.

Prosciutto cotto: Like prosciutto, this is made from pork leg, but the leg is cooked slowly rather than cured. It is often seasoned with herbs and spices and usually thinly sliced, like deli ham.

Soppressata: Made from coarsely ground pork, this dry cured salami is produced in several Italian regions. It can be hot or "sweet" and is typically studded with bits of fat.

FLOURS AND GRAINS

Italians classify their flour as 1, 0, or 00, according to how finely milled it is and how much of the husk and grain of the wheat have been removed. "00" flour is very finely milled and is used for making certain types of pasta. "00" flour with a high protein content is used for pizza dough. Since Italian flour isn't always readily available, and figuring out which to use can be confusing, other, more readily available types can be substituted.

All-purpose flour: Made from a mixture of hard and soft wheats, all-purpose flour can be used to make bread, cakes, pasta, and pizza. I prefer unbleached all-purpose flour over chemically bleached flour.

Bread flour: Made from hard wheat, bread flour has a higher protein content than all-purpose flour. The greater protein translates to gluten development, which produces the elasticity needed in bread baking.

Farro: Grown primarily in central Italy, farro has a nutty, wheatlike flavor and high protein content. It is used in soups and salads and can be ground into flour for making bread and pasta.

Polenta: Both yellow and white polenta (cornmeal) are available in Italy, though yellow is more common. It comes in grinds from fine to coarse. I use finely ground for baking and a mix of fine and medium grind for cooking.

Rice: Several types of short-grain rice are cultivated in northern Italy. The most widely known are Arborio, Carnaroli, and Vialone Nano. They vary somewhat in grain size, texture, and starch content, but all are suitable for risotto and other Italian rice preparations.

Semola rimacinata (fine semolina flour): Semola rimacinata, which means "re-ground," is a fine grind of semolina flour. That is what is called for in the recipes in this book. Semola rimacinata makes excellent fresh pasta, especially rustic southern-style shapes, such as cavatelli (page 56). It is also called for in some bread and pizza doughs. If possible, use a scale to measure the amount of flour used in recipes, as volume (cup) measurements are less accurate. If using cups, lightly spoon the flour into the cup and sweep off the excess with a metal spatula.

HERBS

I mostly use fresh herbs, but occasionally, when a specific recipe calls for it, I use dried. Recipes in this book rely on a variety of herbs common in Italian cooking: basil, bay leaf, marjoram, mint, oregano, flat-leaf parsley, rosemary, sage, and thyme. Woodsy herbs, such as rosemary and sage, are added in the beginning of the cooking process, while tender herbs, such as basil and mint, are generally stirred in at the end.

TOMATOES

In summer, I buy ripe plum tomatoes for adding to soups and for making fresh sauce. But when tomatoes are out of season, I prefer canned tomatoes to the mealy, flavorless ones from the produce bin at the supermarket.

Canned: Whole or chopped canned tomatoes go into soups, stews, and sauces. San Marzano, a variety of sauce tomato grown on the slopes of Mount Vesuvius, in southern Italy, is widely acknowledged as the gold standard due to its meaty texture and full flavor. Look for Italian brands of San Marzano tomatoes, or choose

a U.S. brand of canned plum tomatoes that is consistently good. Always select tomatoes that taste fresh and are canned in their own juice rather than heavy purée.

Passata (purée): Tomato passata, or purée, is a shortcut to a quick, delicious sauce. It is raw (or barely cooked) tomato purée that has been strained of seeds and skin. I like bottled passata, but aseptic-packaged passata in cartons, such as Pomì brand, are also good. Again, choose a brand whose product is unseasoned and tastes fresh and juicy rather than cooked or pasty.

NUTS

It's important to remember that nuts have a shelf life and are perishable. If they are kept around too long, their oils become rancid, and their flavor goes off. Once you've opened a bag of nuts, store leftovers, tightly wrapped, in the freezer to prolong freshness. Almonds, hazelnuts, pistachios, and walnuts are all common in Italian cooking and baking. Nut flours are sometimes used in place of ground nuts in baking. The flours tend to be "drier," with less oil, and when substituted for ground nuts, will sometimes affect the texture of a finished cake or cookie.

OLIVE OIL

For Italians, olive oil is almost as essential as the air they breathe, so quality matters. Stay away from industrially produced oil and find a purveyor you trust to help you choose a high-quality product (three good online purveyors are olio2go.com, gustiamo.com, and olioveto.com). I use more mild-flavored oil, or oil from the previous year's harvest, for cooking, and more assertive, grassy oil for drizzling on soups and dressing salads. Freshly pressed *olio nuovo*, or new-harvest oil, is

the first olive oil to come off the press every fall. It is bottled and enjoyed immediately, rather than being stored for a few months, to allow sediment to settle and the flavor to mellow. It is a luxury worth splurging on once a year for its "green" tomato flavor and peppery bite. Use it for Bread with Olive Oil and Tomatoes (page 12) and the Sliced Steak with Cherry Tomato Confit (page 116).

OLIVES

The bitter fruit of a hardy tree, olives must be cured before they can be eaten. Brine-cured olives stay plump and relatively firm and lose much, but not all, of their bitterness during the extended brining process. Salt- or oil-cured olives become wrinkled, slightly dry, and pleasantly bitter. I keep a small selection of olives in my refrigerator for snacking on and for serving with appetizers. Taggiasca olives, small, brownish olives grown in Liguria, are among my favorites for their delicate, buttery flavor.

SPICES

Spices contribute an additional layer of flavor to many of the recipes in this book. In general, whole spices keep longer than ground spices.

Aniseed: Tiny seeds with a sweet flavor reminiscent of licorice, fennel, and star anise.

Nutmeg: I have a small nutmeg grater that I use to grate whole nutmeg.

Saffron: This precious spice is the red-gold stigma of a variety of crocus. It is sold either in threads or in packets as a powder. The powder dissolves more easily but is also easily tampered with. To be sure you are getting pure saffron, buy the threads (sold in small glass bottles or vials) and gently pound them to a powder before using.

Sea salt: Typically, I use sea salt for cooking and seasoning, coarse sea salt to salt pasta water, and fine sea salt for seasoning most everything else. I also keep a small jar of flaky salt at hand for sprinkling on grilled meats, sliced tomatoes, and cooked vegetables.

Peperoncino (chile): Every spring, I plant a chile pepper plant that flourishes all summer and gives me small, potent peppers. I use some while they're still fresh, snipping or mincing them and stirring them into soups and sauces. I dry the rest, and then grind them in a food processor. Stored in a tightly lidded jar, the ground chile keeps its bright red color and heat for up to a year.

Pepper: I buy whole black peppercorns and grind them in a pepper mill or crush them with a mortar and pestle. Pepper that is freshly ground or crushed is much more potent and flavorful than ground pepper sold in a shaker.

VINEGARS

Red wine vinegar and white wine vinegar are essential in Italian cooking and preserving and for dressing salads and cooked vegetables. Look for high-quality vinegar, preferably aged naturally in wood. The flavor should be bright and aromatic.

Balsamic vinegar: *Aceto balsamico tradizionale* comes from Emilia-Romagna and is made from the cooked must of Trebbiano and Lambrusco grapes. The finest examples are aged for at least twelve years in a series of successively smaller wooden barrels made from different types of wood. As the vinegar ages, it mellows and sweetens, taking on flavors from the wood. There are lots of impostor balsamic vinegars, so find a reliable purveyor and expect to pay for quality.

Bitter lemon vinegar: Produced by Keepwell Vinegar, a small Pennsylvania-based company that makes a variety of artisanal vinegars, this pleasantly bitter vinegar is made from wild, seedy lemons that grow in the mid-Atlantic. I use it in the Bitter Lemon Vinegroni (page 28), though it can also be used in sauces and dressings.

OTHER PANTRY STAPLES

Anchovies: Use high-quality anchovies (either whole or fillets) packed in olive oil or salt. I almost always use Rizzoli brand *alici in salsa piccante*. They are expensive but worth the occasional splurge. Look for them online.

Bomba Calabrese: This spicy condiment, marketed as an antipasto spread, is made from finely chopped vegetables and hot pepper preserved in oil. It is called for in only one recipe in this book, but I often stir a dollop or two into tomato sauce or plain pasta simply dressed with anchovies, garlic, and olive oil. There are a variety of brands available online; my preferred is Delizie di Calabria.

Capers: The preserved buds of a wild shrub, capers have a piquant flavor that brightens many dishes. Capers packed in sea salt retain their intense floral flavor and firm texture, but vinegar-brined capers are less expensive and more commonly available. Rinse both types before using.

Giardiniera: I make my own *giardiniera* (pickled mixed vegetables) every fall. But when I run out, I use imported bottled *giardiniera* packed in vinegar and olive oil.

ACKNOWLEDGEMENTS

Heartfelt thanks to the talented team who produced this book: associate publisher Amy Marr, editors Jourdan Plautz and Sharon Silva, designer Debbie Berne, proofreader Rachel Markowitz, photographer Erin Scott, food stylist Lillian Kang, and prop stylist Emma Star Jensen. Thanks also to my husband, Scott Vance, for the cocktail contributions, and to Scott, Nick, and Adriana, as always, for their support.

INDEX

EVERYDAY ITALIAN COOKBOOK

Conceived and produced by Weldon Owen International
in collaboration with Williams Sonoma, Inc.
3250 Van Ness Avenue, San Francisco, CA 94109

A Weldon Owen Production
PO Box 3088
San Rafael, CA 94912
www.weldonowen.com

Library of Congress Cataloging-in-
Publication data is available.

ISBN-13: 979-8-88674-003-5

Manufactured in China by Insight Editions
10 9 8 7 6 5 4 3 2

weldon**owen**

CEO Raoul Goff
Publisher Roger Shaw
Associate Publisher Amy Marr
Editorial Director Katie Killebrew
Assistant Editor Jourdan Plautz
VP of Creative Chrissy Kwasnik
Design Manager Megan Sinead Harris
Production Manager Josh Smith

Designer Debbie Berne
Photographer Erin Scott
Food Stylist Lillian Kang
Prop Stylist Emma Star Jensen

Weldon Owen wishes to thank the following people for their generous support
in producing this book: Rachel Markowitz, Elizabeth Parson, and Sharon Silva.

Insight Editions, in association with Roots of Peace, will plant two trees for each
tree used in the manufacturing of this book. Roots of Peace is an internationally
renowned humanitarian organization dedicated to eradicating land mines
worldwide and converting war-torn lands into productive farms and wildlife
habitats. Roots of Peace will plant two million fruit and nut trees in Afghanistan and
provide farmers there with the skills and support necessary for sustainable land use.